THE HOMESTEAD to TABLE

COOKBOOK

GEORGIA VAROZZA

TEN PEAKS PRESS®
EUGENE, OR

CONTENTS

THE HOMESTEAD-TO-TABLE EXPERIENCE IS FOR EVERYONE

When you hear the word *homestead*, do you immediately think of sturdy pioneers who wrest a self-sufficient living from bare land, build their homes from the materials on hand, and eat only what they can harvest, hunt, or forage? Or perhaps your vision is of a solar powered, off-grid home with a low carbon footprint, the residents eating only locally sourced food. Maybe you live in a city or the suburbs and have planter boxes overflowing with herbs and spices, tomatoes and spinach, barely making a dent in your food budget yet enhancing each meal with the flavor of homegrown offerings and the satisfaction of savoring what you've harvested.

I'm a firm believer that homesteading is many things and happens in many ways. After all, homesteading begins with the word *home*—a word that houses unique meaning for each of us. So, keep the spirit of homesteading alive and express it any way that suits you.

No matter how you or I define *homestead*, food is a must-have part of the experience. We all need to eat. And while living busy lives we've built around self-reliance, we often find ourselves needing a meal in a hurry. When you use the recipes in this book, think quick and easy. Even if an ingredient isn't something you've grown or raised, there's a good chance it is a basic in your cupboard. Who has time to run to the store to get some special item just to finish making dinner? Not you and not me, because we're too busy taking charge of our lives and caring for our little corner of the universe. It's a satisfying endeavor, for sure.

Explore these recipes. Decide what works for you today. Choose textures and tastes that delight, cook ingredients that fill the kitchen with pleasing aromas, and serve meals that will satisfy and nourish those at your table. And tomorrow when you awake, decide anew what works and then do that. Each day dawns with opportunities to fashion a life and a meal of our own making. This journey is wonderfully personal—just like home.

Ah, breakfast. It's the most important meal of the day. Our bodies need that early morning sustenance for energy to see us through the day. It seems to be a modern notion that we can haul ourselves out of bed at the last minute, rush around getting ready for the day, and then leave home without stopping long enough to eat a proper breakfast . . . and yet somehow manage to perform flawlessly.

Not so. Do yourself and your family a favor and sit down to a decent breakfast. You'll be so glad you did.

In this section you'll find lots to choose from. Some of the recipes can be started the night before, some are quick and easy, and others take a bit more time.

Let's get started the right way.

Baked Oatmeal

1 cup oil
⅔ cup brown sugar or slightly
  more than ½ cup honey
6 eggs

6 cups rolled oats
3 tsp. baking powder
2 tsp. salt
2 cups milk

Preheat the oven to 350°.

Mix together the oil, sugar or honey, and eggs. Add the oats, baking powder, salt, and milk; mix well.

Pour the batter into a lightly buttered 13 x 9-inch baking pan and bake in the preheated oven for 30 minutes.

Place the warm baked oatmeal in a bowl and top with warm milk, cinnamon, and brown sugar.

Baked oatmeal is especially favored by children.

Serves 8

Note: *This can be mixed the night before.*

Bread Omelet

½ loaf day-old bread, cut into cubes
½ cup butter
3 eggs, slightly beaten

½ cup milk
Salt and pepper to taste

In a large frying pan, melt the butter over medium heat, then add the bread cubes and brown them in the butter.

Mix together the eggs, milk, salt, and pepper. Pour the egg mixture over the bread cubes and fry until the eggs are cooked through.

This is a perfect recipe for the frugal at heart!

Serves 4 to 6

Measure and mix the dry ingredients for a breakfast recipe the night before. It saves precious time in the morning when the family is busy getting ready for the day.

Buttermilk Oatmeal Pancakes

....

Start the night before.

2 cups rolled oats	1½ tsp. baking soda
2 cups buttermilk, plus a bit more if needed	1 tsp. salt
1 cup flour	2 eggs
2 tsp. sugar	2 T. butter, melted and cooled slightly
1½ tsp. baking powder	

In a mixing bowl, combine the oats and buttermilk. Cover and refrigerate overnight.

In another mixing bowl, mix together the flour, sugar, baking powder, baking soda, and salt. Cover and set aside overnight.

The next morning, remove the oat mixture from the refrigerator and set aside.

In a large mixing bowl, whisk the eggs until they are light and frothy. Add the melted butter and whisk again. Next, add the oats and mix well. Blend in the flour mixture; you will need to stir with a large wooden spoon at this point because the mixture will be very thick. If it appears too dry, you can add a few more tablespoons of buttermilk.

Fry the pancakes in a greased frying pan or griddle, turning once and cooking well on both sides. These pancakes really puff up, so it's better to cook them on a bit lower heat than usual but for a longer time so they have a chance to cook completely.

Serve them hot from the griddle with butter and maple syrup.

Serves 6

Cinnamon French Toast

....

4 eggs	Pinch of nutmeg (optional)
⅔ cup milk	2 T. butter, more or less
1 tsp. ground cinnamon	2 T. light flavored oil, more or less
Pinch of salt	8 slices bread, sliced thick

In a medium mixing bowl, beat together the eggs, milk, cinnamon, salt, and nutmeg until well blended. Pour the mixture into a container that has a flat bottom and is large enough to accommodate a piece of bread laid flat. (I use a large pie plate or casserole dish.)

Melt the butter with the oil on medium-low heat in a skillet or frying pan. If your skillet is small, you may need to separate the butter and oil into smaller batches before heating them in the pan. Then use some with each batch as you fry your bread.

Dip each slice of bread into the egg mixture, allowing time for the bread to soak a bit. Place the bread slices into the skillet, being careful to keep the bread from overlapping other pieces or being too crowded, which will make it easier to flip. Fry the French toast on both sides until each side is golden brown and the egg mixture is cooked in the middle.

If you cook the French toast in batches, keep the cooked slices warm while frying the remaining bread. Serve immediately with your favorite toppings, such as maple syrup, fresh fruit, powdered sugar, or honey.

Serves 4 (2 pieces each)

No buttermilk? No problem. You can substitute 1 cup of buttermilk with 1 cup of regular milk mixed with 1 tablespoon of white vinegar or lemon juice. Here's how: Pour the vinegar into a liquid measuring cup and then add milk to the 1-cup fill line. Stir the mixture and let it sit for 5 minutes until it curdles slightly. Then it will be ready to use with a recipe just as buttermilk would be used.

Coffee Cake

CAKE
1¼ cups flour
½ cup sugar
2 tsp. baking powder
½ tsp. salt
½ cup milk
1 egg
3 T. butter, melted and cooled

TOPPING
¼ cup brown sugar
¼ cup chopped nuts
1 T. flour
2 tsp. ground cinnamon
1 T. butter, room temperature

Preheat the oven to 375°.

For the cinnamon nut topping:

In a small mixing bowl, mix together the brown sugar, chopped nuts, flour, and cinnamon. Add the butter and mix together until the mixture resembles coarse crumbs, then set aside.

For the coffee cake:

In a large mixing bowl, stir together the flour, sugar, baking powder, and salt. Pour the milk into another bowl, then whisk in the egg and the melted butter. Pour all at once into the flour mixture and stir until just combined. Pour the batter into a greased 8 x 8-inch baking dish. Sprinkle the cinnamon nut topping over the top of the batter and bake for 20 to 25 minutes or until baked through.

Serves 6 to 8

Using room-temperature eggs ensures that your baked goods will be lighter and fluffier than when using eggs straight from the fridge. Set the eggs out at room temperature for about 30 minutes to warm them.

Cottage Cheese Pancakes

1 cup cottage cheese
4 eggs
½ cup flour
¼ tsp. salt

¼ cup oil
½ cup milk
½ tsp. vanilla extract (optional)

Mix together all the ingredients until they are well blended and the batter is smooth, although there will still be small lumps of cottage cheese. Fry on a lightly greased griddle or frying pan over medium heat, leaving plenty of room between pancakes for turning. You will need to turn the pancakes quickly because the batter is thin, but you'll soon get the hang of it.

If you've ever eaten cheese blintzes or crepes, these pancakes will prove reminiscent. These delicate pancakes make for an excellent light brunch or lunch when paired with a tossed green salad or fruit. You can also try them rolled around a bit of blackberry jam and sprinkled with powdered sugar.

Serves 6

Crustless Vegetable Quiche

1 lb. fresh baby spinach or 1 (10 oz.) box
  frozen spinach, thawed
⅓ cup mushrooms, sliced
⅓ cup onion, diced
⅓ cup bell pepper, diced
1 clove garlic, minced

4 eggs
1 cup milk
Salt and pepper to taste
1 cup shredded cheese (cheddar, Swiss, or Gruyère)
2 T. Parmesan cheese

Preheat the oven to 350°.

If you are using fresh spinach, sauté it until wilted, then rinse it in cool water and squeeze it dry. If you are using previously frozen spinach, rinse it and squeeze it dry.

Lightly butter or grease a 10-inch pie pan; place the prepared spinach in the bottom of the pan. Set aside.

In a sauté pan, cook the mushrooms, onion, bell pepper, and garlic in a bit of oil or butter (or use a nonstick sauté pan) until the vegetables are softened slightly. Place the vegetables on top of the spinach in the pie pan.

In a medium mixing bowl, whisk together the eggs, milk, salt, and pepper, then pour the mixture over the vegetables in the pie pan. Next, sprinkle the cheese evenly across the top of the egg mixture.

Bake for 45 to 55 minutes or until the quiche is set and the top is golden.

Serves 6 to 8

Note: *This reheats very well in the microwave and also makes a great light lunch dish served with a green salad.*

German Egg Pancakes

5 eggs, separated
½ cup milk
1 cup flour

In a large mixing bowl, beat the egg yolks until very light. Add the milk and flour gradually, mixing well after each addition. Mix until the batter is smooth. In another large bowl, beat the egg whites until they are stiff. Fold the whites gently into the batter.

Drop large spoonfuls of batter on a hot greased griddle or frying pan, turning once to cook both sides. Serve hot, sprinkled with powdered sugar or spread with jam.

Serves 6

Dutch Babies

½ cup flour
½ tsp. salt
4 eggs

½ cup milk
2 to 3 T. butter, softened

Preheat the oven to 400°.

Place a cast-iron pot or deep-sided oven-proof frying pan in the oven while it is preheating.

In a small bowl, stir together the flour and salt. In a large mixing bowl, beat the eggs thoroughly. Alternately add the flour mixture and the milk to the eggs, beating well after each addition to form a smooth batter.

Being careful not to burn yourself, remove the cast-iron pot or frying pan from the oven. Spread the softened butter on the bottom and up the sides of the cast-iron pot. Pour the egg batter into the pot or frying pan and set in the oven. Bake for 5 minutes and then turn down the heat to 350° and bake for another 15 to 20 minutes or until the pancake is puffed up the sides of the pan and is crisp and golden on the top.

Serve plain or with powdered sugar or maple syrup. Gather the kids around when you take this out of the oven because the puffed "baby" is something to behold.

Serves 6

Easy Apple Fritters

1 cup flour
1½ tsp. baking powder
2 T. sugar
½ tsp. salt

¾ cup milk
1 egg
4 large apples
Shortening for frying

In a medium bowl, mix together the flour, baking powder, sugar, and salt. Add the milk and the egg and beat the batter until it is smooth.

Peel and core the apples and slice them into rings about ¼ inch thick.

Melt the shortening in a heavy-duty deep-sided skillet (cast iron works well); you want the melted shortening to be about ½-inch deep. Dip the apple rings into the batter and gently drop them into the skillet. Fry each slice until golden brown, turning once so both sides are cooked. Drain the fritters on paper towels and then sprinkle them liberally with cinnamon sugar.

The number of fritters you will get varies depending on the size of your apples.

Graham "Nuts" Cereal

3½ cups whole wheat flour	1 tsp. ground cinnamon
1 cup brown sugar	2 cups buttermilk
1 tsp. salt	2 tsp. vanilla extract
1 tsp. baking soda	

Preheat the oven to 350°.

In a large bowl, combine all the ingredients and mix well. Pour onto an oiled 12 x 16-inch low-sided baking pan, such as a jelly roll pan, and spread evenly with a spatula. Bake for 20 minutes or until the batter is firm and has begun to shrink away slightly from the sides of the pan. With a spatula, completely loosen the hot "cake" and allow it to cool on a rack for several hours.

Once the cake has cooled, preheat the oven to 275°.

Break the cake into chunks and pass each piece through a coarse-bladed meat grinder or through a food screen or colander that has ¼-inch grids. Divide the crumbs between two 12 x 16-inch baking pans.

Bake the crumbs for 30 minutes, stirring every 10 minutes. Let the trays of crumbs cool completely, then remove the cereal and place it in airtight containers to store.

Serve as a cold cereal with milk, use as a topping for a fruit crisp, or sprinkle on yogurt or ice cream. This cereal will keep in your pantry for a month or longer, depending on how dry the baked cereal is.

Yield: a bit more than one quart of cereal

Granola

2 cups whole wheat flour	½ cup water
6 cups rolled oats	1 cup oil
1 cup coconut	1 cup honey
1 cup wheat germ	2 tsp. vanilla extract
1 T. salt	

Combine the dry ingredients in a large mixing bowl. Blend the liquid ingredients, then add to the bowl and mix thoroughly. Spread the mixture out on 2 greased cookie sheets or jelly roll pans and bake at 250°, stirring occasionally, for 1 hour or until dry and golden.

Cool the granola completely, then store in an airtight container.

You can also add nuts, sunflower seeds, or raisins, if desired. Also, I often omit the wheat germ, increase the flour a wee bit, and call it good. We never seem to miss it.

Yield: at least ½ gallon

If you'll be baking something for an hour or more, there's no need to preheat the oven.

When cracking raw eggs, crack like you mean business. Too tentative of a crack causes the shell to shatter into small pieces, making it more likely that eggshell could get in your bowl. But if that happens? Simply fish out the unwanted shell bit by using half of the eggshell to scoop it up. Alternatively, you can wet a finger and scoop the broken piece of shell out of the bowl.

Hush Puppies

1 cup cornmeal
1 tsp. baking powder
½ tsp. salt
1 egg

½ cup milk (may need a bit more)
4 slices bacon (optional)
Oil for frying

If you are using bacon, cut it up and fry it. When you remove it from the pan, leave the grease in the pan to use for frying the hush puppies.

In a large bowl, mix together the dry ingredients. In another bowl, mix together the egg and the milk and then add them to the dry ingredients; mix well. If using bacon, add it now and mix well again.

Reheat the bacon grease or heat a shallow layer of oil in a frying pan over medium-high heat. (Hush puppies soak up the grease, so make sure the pan is liberally coated before dropping in the batter; you may need to add a bit more before the entire batch has been cooked.) Drop large spoonfuls of batter into the pan and fry until golden brown. Remove the hush puppies to a plate or pan lined with a paper towel.

To determine if an egg is still fresh, gently place it in a container that is filled with water. If the egg stays at the bottom of the container on its side, the egg is fresh. If the egg stays at the bottom of the container but tips upright, the egg is edible but not as fresh. However, if the egg rises to the top of the water, it is no longer fresh enough to eat.

Serve immediately just as they are or with maple syrup.

Makes 12 hush puppies

Layered Breakfast Casserole

12 slices bread
1 lb. thinly sliced ham, divided
2 cups shredded cheddar cheese, divided
6 large eggs
3 cups milk
1 tsp. dry mustard powder

1 tsp. onion powder
½ tsp. salt
½ tsp. pepper
¼ cup butter, melted
2 cups cornflakes, crushed (optional)

Preheat the oven to 350°.

Grease a 9 x 13-inch baking dish and line it with 6 slices of bread. Layer half of the ham over the bread and sprinkle with half of the cheese. Repeat these layers one more time.

In a large mixing bowl, combine the eggs, milk, dry mustard, onion powder, salt, and pepper and mix well. Slowly pour the egg mixture evenly over the bread layers in the baking dish.

Mix the melted butter with the cornflakes and sprinkle evenly over the top of the casserole. Since I rarely have cornflakes, I often forego this ingredient. However, I do melt a couple of tablespoons of butter and drizzle it on top of the casserole before I bake it.

Bake 45 to 50 minutes or until set.

Serves 8

Omelet Roll

2 tsp. butter	½ tsp. salt
¼ cup onion, finely diced	¼ tsp. pepper
12 eggs	½ lb. ham, thinly sliced
½ tsp. ground mustard powder	½ lb. Swiss cheese, sliced

Preheat the oven to 350°.

Lightly grease the bottom and sides of a large jelly roll pan (at least 10 x 15 inches). Line the greased pan with parchment paper and grease the paper as well.

In a sauté pan, melt the butter and add the diced onion. Cook until the onion is limp. Remove the onion to a mixing bowl and combine with the eggs, mustard powder, salt, and pepper and whisk well. Pour the mixture into the prepared pan and bake for 10 to 15 minutes or until the omelet is set.

Remove the omelet from the oven and invert it onto a piece of aluminum foil; gently peel off the parchment paper. Layer the omelet with the ham and Swiss cheese and then roll it up jelly roll fashion, starting with the short side, and wrap the roll tightly in aluminum foil.

Place the roll on a cookie sheet and return it to the oven for 10 minutes. When baked, remove the foil, slice the omelet into thick rolls, and serve.

Serves 8

Potato Pancakes

3 eggs	¼ cup milk
6 T. flour	5 or 6 medium-sized potatoes
1 tsp. salt	Lard or shortening for frying

In a large bowl, beat the eggs and then add the flour, salt, and milk and whisk to combine.

Peel the raw potatoes and then grate them coarsely. Work quickly so the potatoes don't darken and get starchy. Add the grated potatoes to the egg mixture and stir to mix.

Heat 3 to 4 tablespoons of lard or shortening in a large frying pan and let it melt. Ladle a small amount of the pancake batter (it will be rather runny) into the frying pan and spread each pancake so it's thin. Fry the batter quickly, turning each pancake over when the first side is crisp and golden. Cook the second side until it is crisp and golden as well.

These pancakes are best eaten as soon as they come out of the pan.

Serves 6 to 8

Pumpkin Pancakes

1 cup flour
⅛ tsp. baking soda
2 T. sugar
¼ tsp. cinnamon
⅛ tsp. ginger
⅛ tsp. nutmeg

1 egg, beaten
1¼ cups milk
2 T. melted shortening, butter, or vegetable oil
½ cup canned pumpkin (you can also use
cooked and mashed sweet potato or delicata
squash)

In a large mixing bowl, combine the flour, baking soda, sugar, and spices.

In a medium bowl, combine the egg, milk, melted shortening, and pumpkin. Add this to the flour mixture and beat well until smooth.

Ladle a small amount of batter onto a preheated, lightly greased griddle or frying pan, turning once. Serve the pancakes plain, with butter and maple syrup, or with powdered sugar.

Pumpkin pancakes are just the thing on a cold winter morning.

Serves 6

Sausage and Egg Casserole

Start the night before.

1 lb. bulk pork sausage	1 tsp. salt
6 eggs	6 slices bread, cubed
1 tsp. dry mustard powder	4 oz. cheddar cheese, cubed or shredded
2 cups milk	

Brown the sausage and drain off the grease. Beat the eggs in a large bowl, then add the mustard, milk, and salt. Mix in the bread cubes, cheese, and sausage. Pour the mixture into a buttered 9 x 13-inch or 10 x 15-inch baking dish. Cover the dish with plastic wrap and refrigerate overnight.

In the morning, take the casserole out of the refrigerator and let it sit on the counter for a half hour while preheating the oven to 350°. Bake the casserole for 45 to 55 minutes or until set. (If you use the smaller baking dish, you'll need to bake it for the longer time.) Remove the pan from the oven and let it set for several minutes before cutting.

This dish always gets raves and is so easy to prepare.

Serves 6 to 8

Scrambled Egg and Ham Bake

SAUCE	FILLING	TOPPING
1 T. butter	2 T. butter	2 to 3 T. butter, melted
1½ T. flour	¾ cup cubed ham	1 heaping cup soft bread crumbs
1 cup milk	⅛ to ¼ cup onion, diced	
¼ tsp. salt	(can use green onion if desired)	
Pinch of pepper	6 eggs, whisked	
½ to 1 cup shredded cheddar cheese		

Preheat the oven to 350°.

For the cheese sauce:

In a medium saucepan, melt the butter and then blend in the flour. Slowly pour in the milk, stirring constantly until the mixture has bubbled and thickened. Add the salt, pepper, and cheese and continue stirring until the cheese has melted completely. Set aside.

For the filling:

In large frying pan, melt the butter. Add the ham and onion and sauté until the onion is tender. Add the whisked eggs and cook, stirring, until the eggs are set. Stir in the cheese sauce and remove the pan from the heat.

For the topping:

In a small bowl, add the bread crumbs to the melted butter and mix well.

Grease a 9 x 9-inch baking dish and spoon the egg and cheese mixture evenly into the pan. Sprinkle the topping mixture evenly over the top of the eggs. Bake the casserole for about 20 minutes or until topping has browned nicely.

Serves 6

Waffles

3 eggs, separated
2 cups flour, sifted
2 slightly heaped tsp. baking powder
2 tsp. sugar

¼ tsp. salt
5 T. butter, melted and cooled
1½ cups milk

In a medium bowl, beat the egg whites until stiff, then set aside. In a large mixing bowl, whisk together the yolks and set aside.

Sift the flour before measuring and then sift together the flour, baking powder, sugar, and salt. (Sifting twice will help make your waffles light and fluffy.)

Alternately add the flour mixture and the milk to the egg yolks, mixing well. Add the melted butter and mix again. Last, fold in the stiffly beaten egg whites.

Cook the waffles in a lightly oiled waffle iron.

Makes about 8 waffles

Comfort food. That's what biscuits are to me. With a dollop of butter, honey, or jam, biscuits add that perfect touch to almost any meal. Even better? Biscuits are quick and easy to make, and the payoff in taste more than makes up for the little bit of effort and minimal ingredients required to make them.

I often make biscuits when I need something to add to a meal at the last minute. When that's the case, I'll simply make the dough, add a splash or two of extra liquid so they are a bit on the soft side, and then drop the dough in rough mounds onto my baking sheet instead of going to the trouble of rolling them out and cutting them. It saves even more time, and even though they may not look as pretty as the rolled-out version, my drop biscuits taste just as good. Really, you can't go wrong when biscuits are on the menu.

I hope you find something new in this chapter to add to your tried-and-true buttermilk biscuits. Give a few of these recipes a try and see if you discover a new family favorite.

BISCUITS AND SCONES

Master Biscuit Mix

....

8½ cups flour
3 T. baking powder
1 T. salt
2 tsp. cream of tartar

1 tsp. baking soda
1½ cups instant nonfat dry milk
2¼ cups shortening

In a large mixing bowl, sift together all the dry ingredients, blending well. With a pastry blender, cut in the shortening until it is evenly distributed and the consistency of coarse cornmeal. Place the mix in an airtight container or large plastic storage bags. Store in a cool, dry place. Date the container and use within 3 months.

This Master Biscuit Mix can be used in place of Bisquick in many recipes. I store my Master Biscuit Mix in a gallon jar with a tight-fitting lid and keep it in my pantry.

Basic Biscuits

2 cups all-purpose flour
4 tsp. baking powder
½ tsp. salt

⅓ cup shortening
¾ cup milk

Preheat the oven to 450°.

In a large bowl, sift together the flour, baking powder, and salt. Cut in the shortening until the mixture resembles coarse crumbs. Make a well in the center of the flour and pour the milk into the well all at once. Stir the dough with a fork until it comes clean from the sides of the bowl.

Turn out the dough onto a lightly floured surface and knead it gently about 10 times. Roll or pat the dough to ½-inch thickness and cut the biscuits using a biscuit cutter or the top of a glass that has been dredged in flour to prevent the dough from sticking to the glass. Place the biscuits on an ungreased baking sheet about 1 inch apart. Bake for 15 to 20 minutes or until the tops are starting to brown slightly and they are fully baked.

Makes 10 biscuits

Note: *To make drop biscuits, add an extra ¼ cup of milk to the dough, then instead of kneading and cutting out the biscuits, simply drop heaping spoonfuls of dough onto a greased baking sheet and bake for 15 to 20 minutes or until done.*

After cutting out your circles of biscuit dough, pat together the small pieces of dough left over and make another biscuit or two. Even though these biscuits made from scraps may be misshapen, they taste just as good as the prettier ones.

Angel Buttermilk Biscuits

4½ tsp. (2 packages) active dry yeast
¼ cup warm water (about 110°)
2 cups warm buttermilk (about 110°)
5 cups all-purpose flour
⅓ cup sugar

2 tsp. salt
2 tsp. baking powder
1 tsp. baking soda
1 cup shortening
Melted butter for brushing

In a small bowl, stir together the yeast and warm water. Let it stand for 5 minutes, then stir in the warm buttermilk. Set aside.

In a large bowl, combine the flour, sugar, salt, baking powder, and baking soda. Cut in the shortening until the mixture resembles coarse cornmeal.

Stir the yeast mixture into the dry ingredients.

Turn out the dough onto a lightly floured surface and knead it gently for about 30 seconds. Roll out the dough to a ½-inch thickness and cut it with a biscuit cutter. Place the biscuits on a lightly greased baking sheet with their sides not quite touching. Cover the biscuits and let them rise until doubled, about 30 to 45 minutes. Meanwhile, preheat the oven to 450°.

Bake for 8 to 10 minutes or until done. When you remove them from the oven, immediately brush the tops with melted butter.

Makes about 24 biscuits

Buttermilk Orange Scones

3 cups flour
½ cup granulated sugar
½ tsp. baking soda
1 T. baking powder
¼ tsp. salt
1½ tsp. grated orange or lemon zest
½ cup very cold butter

1 cup dried cranberries or blueberries
1 cup chopped walnuts or pecans
1 cup buttermilk
Small amount of heavy cream
Small amount of coarse sugar

Preheat the oven to 400°.

In a large mixing bowl, blend the flour, sugar, baking soda, baking powder, salt, and zest. Cut the butter into the flour mixture until it resembles coarse crumbs. Stir in the dried berries and nuts. Add the buttermilk and mix with a fork until a soft dough forms, being careful not to overmix.

Pat the dough into a 1-inch-thick circle. Brush the top of the dough with the cream and then sprinkle with the coarse sugar.

Cut the dough into 12 pieces and place them on a cookie sheet that has been greased or lined with a silicone baking mat or parchment paper. Let stand for 10 minutes.

Bake for 12 to 15 minutes or until done.

Makes 12 scones

Note: *You can buy dried orange or lemon zest in the spice aisle at many grocery stores, but freshly grated zest elevates the taste. Using a microplane grater, simply grate the peel of the orange or lemon, being careful to only grate the peel and not the white pith, which can be bitter.*

Cheesy Bacon Drop Biscuits

2 cups all-purpose flour
4 tsp. baking powder
½ tsp. salt
5 T. shortening

⅓ cup shredded cheddar cheese
4 to 6 slices bacon, cooked and crumbled
1 cup milk

Preheat the oven to 450°.

In a large bowl, mix together the flour, baking powder, and salt. Cut in the shortening until the mixture resembles coarse crumbs. Mix in the cheese and bacon. Make a well in the center of the dough and pour in the milk all at once. Stir with a fork until the dough is mixed thoroughly and sticks mostly together in a soft ball.

Drop heaping tablespoons of dough onto a greased baking sheet and bake for 15 to 20 minutes or until done.

Makes about 12 biscuits

Cheesy Garlic Biscuits

BISCUITS
2 cups homemade biscuit mix
   (see page 28) or Bisquick
⅔ cup milk
⅔ cup shredded cheddar cheese

TOPPING
⅓ cup butter
¼ tsp. garlic powder, more or less to taste
¼ heaping tsp. dried parsley
A few shakes of salt
Shake of pepper

Preheat the oven to 400°.

For the biscuits:

In a medium bowl, stir together the biscuit mix, milk, and cheddar cheese; don't overmix.

Drop large spoonfuls of dough onto an ungreased cookie sheet or a cookie sheet lined with a silicone baking mat. Bake the biscuits for about 10 minutes or until they are golden on top and completely baked.

For the topping:

While the biscuits are in the oven, melt the butter in a small saucepan over low heat. Add the garlic powder, parsley, salt, and pepper to the butter, and gently stir to mix. Remove the biscuits from the oven, and while they are still on the baking sheet, immediately brush the tops of the biscuits generously with the melted butter mixture.

Makes about 10 biscuits

Cheesy Sausage Biscuits

2 cups all-purpose flour
4 tsp. baking powder
½ tsp. salt
5 T. shortening

⅓ cup shredded cheddar cheese
½ cup ground breakfast sausage, cooked, drained,
   and crumbled
1 cup milk

Preheat the oven to 450°.

In a large bowl, mix together the flour, baking powder, and salt. Cut in the shortening until the mixture resembles coarse crumbs. Stir the cheese and sausage into the flour mixture, then make a well in the center and pour in the milk all at once. Stir the dough with a fork until it is mixed thoroughly and sticks mostly together in a soft ball.

Drop heaping tablespoons of dough onto a greased baking sheet and bake for 15 to 20 minutes or until done.

Makes about 10 biscuits

Chopped Chicken Biscuits

2 cups all-purpose flour
4 tsp. baking powder
½ tsp. salt
3 T. shortening

¾ cup milk
2 cups cooked, chopped chicken (more or less—
    just use what you have)

Preheat the oven to 425°.

In a large bowl, mix together the flour, baking powder, and salt. Cut in the shortening until it resembles coarse crumbs. Add the milk all at once and mix well. Turn out the dough onto a floured work surface and knead about 25 times. Roll out the ball of dough to a ¼-inch-thick rectangle. Cover generously with the chicken. Roll up the dough as you would a jelly roll and slice it into pieces that are about an inch thick. Place them on a greased cookie sheet about an inch apart.

Bake for 15 minutes.

Makes about 10 biscuits

If a recipe calls for shortening, you can replace the shortening with lard.

Cream Cheese Biscuits

2 cups all-purpose flour
1 T. baking powder
1 T. sugar
¾ tsp. salt
3 oz. very cold cream cheese, cut into small pieces

¼ cup shortening
½ cup finely chopped green onion (I've used
    finely minced yellow onion when I didn't have
    green onions)
⅔ cup milk

Preheat the oven to 450°.

In a large bowl, combine the flour, baking powder, sugar, and salt. Cut the cream cheese and shortening into the flour mixture until it resembles coarse crumbs. Stir in the green onions.

Make a well in the center of the flour mixture, add the milk, and stir with a fork to form a soft ball of dough. Turn out the dough onto a floured surface and gently knead it for 30 seconds. Roll or pat the dough to ½-inch thickness and then cut it with a biscuit cutter.

Place the biscuits on an ungreased baking sheet and bake for 10 to 12 minutes or until done.

Makes about 8 biscuits

Cream Scones

2 cups all-purpose flour
3 tsp. baking powder
2 T. plus 2 tsp. sugar, divided
½ tsp. salt

¼ cup (½ stick) butter
2 eggs, one of them separated
⅓ cup whipping cream

Preheat the oven to 400°.

In a large mixing bowl, sift together the flour, baking powder, 2 tablespoons of the sugar, and the salt. Cut in the butter until the mixture resembles coarse crumbs.

In a separate bowl, separate the yolk of one of the eggs, reserving the egg white to brush on the tops of the scones. Stir the yolk together with the other whole egg, then stir in the cream.

Make a well in the center of the flour mixture and pour the egg and cream mixture into the well. Stir with a fork just until the dough pulls away from the sides of the bowl.

Sprinkle a clean surface with a small amount of flour. Using your hands, pat the dough into a ball and knead it on the floured surface for about 30 seconds. Divide the dough ball into 2 equal halves. Roll out each half of the dough into a circle that is about 1 inch thick and about 6 inches in diameter. Cut each circle into 4 pie-shaped wedges and place them on an ungreased baking sheet about 1 inch apart. Brush the tops with the reserved egg white, and then sprinkle the wedges with the remaining 2 teaspoons of sugar.

Bake for 15 minutes or until done but not too dark. The scones are good plain, but they are even better when topped with jam and sweetened whipped cream.

Makes 8 scones

Sweetened Whipped Cream

1 cup heavy cream
1-2 T. granulated sugar, or to taste

½ tsp. vanilla extract

Place all the ingredients into a 1-quart mixing bowl and beat with an electric mixer. Start on medium speed and then increase to high speed when the cream begins to thicken. (This helps to keep the cream from splashing out of the mixing bowl.) Continue beating until peaks form.

Dried Sweet Cherry or Blueberry Biscuits

2 cups all-purpose flour
2 T. sugar
4 tsp. baking powder
½ tsp. salt

½ tsp. dried rosemary
½ cup (1 stick) very cold butter, cut into small pieces
¾ cup milk
½ cup dried cherries or blueberries, chopped

Preheat the oven to 425°.

In a large bowl, mix together the flour, sugar, baking powder, salt, and rosemary. Cut in the butter until the mixture resembles coarse crumbs. Make a well in the center and add the milk, then stir to form a soft dough. Stir in the cherries (or blueberries).

Turn out the dough onto a floured surface and knead for 30 seconds. Roll or pat the dough to 1-inch thickness and then cut with a biscuit cutter. Place the biscuits about 1 inch apart on an ungreased baking sheet (or you can use a silicone baking mat) and bake for 15 minutes or until done.

Makes about 8 biscuits

Ham and Cheese Biscuits

2 cups all-purpose flour
2 tsp. baking powder
½ tsp. baking soda
½ cup (1 stick) very cold butter,
    cut into small pieces

⅔ cup buttermilk
½ cup shredded cheese (Swiss works well)
2 oz. ham, diced (about ⅓ cup)

Preheat the oven to 450°.

In a large bowl, combine the flour, baking powder, and baking soda. Cut in the butter until the mixture resembles coarse crumbs. Add the buttermilk and then stir with a fork to form a soft, sticky dough. Stir in the cheese and ham.

Turn out the dough onto a floured surface and knead for about 30 seconds. Roll or pat the dough to ½-inch thickness and then cut with a biscuit cutter. Place the biscuits 2 inches apart on a baking sheet that has been greased or lined with a silicone baking mat.

Bake for about 10 minutes or until the biscuits are golden brown and done.

Makes about 8 biscuits

Herbed Biscuits

2 cups all-purpose flour	1 tsp. salt	½ tsp. celery seed
2 tsp. baking powder	¼ tsp. dry mustard	¼ cup shortening
¼ tsp. baking soda	½ tsp. dried sage	¾ cup buttermilk

Preheat the oven to 425°.

In a large bowl, mix together the dry ingredients, including the herbs. Cut in the shortening until the mixture resembles coarse crumbs. Add the buttermilk and stir using a fork until a soft dough forms.

Turn out the dough onto a floured surface and knead about 20 times. Roll or pat the dough to a ½-inch thickness and then cut with a biscuit cutter.

Place the biscuits on an ungreased baking sheet and bake for about 10 minutes or until done.

Makes about 8 biscuits

Light-as-Air Biscuits

2 cups all-purpose flour	½ tsp. cream of tartar
½ tsp. salt	½ cup shortening
2 tsp. sugar	⅔ cup milk
4 tsp. baking powder	

Preheat the oven to 450°.

In a large bowl, mix together the flour, salt, sugar, baking powder, and cream of tartar. Cut in the shortening until the mixture resembles coarse crumbs. Make a well in the center and add the milk all at once; stir with a fork until the dough leaves the sides of the bowl.

Turn out the dough onto a lightly floured surface and knead about 5 times. Roll or pat the dough to a ½-inch thickness and then cut with a biscuit cutter.

Place the biscuits on an ungreased baking sheet and bake for 15 minutes or until done.

Makes about 8 biscuits

Biscuits Versus Scones: What's the Difference?

Depending on where you live in the world, this question can be answered in various ways. But where I come from (North America), biscuits are most often made to include buttermilk or butter (or both), and they are moist and flaky. Scones are made with heavy cream and are dense, a tad crumbly, and usually have a bit of sweetener added. Ingredients for both should be cold when you begin, and the dough should be handled with a quick, light hand to prevent the dough from becoming tough.

Maple Nut Scones

....

3½ cups all-purpose flour
1 cup finely chopped nuts (walnuts or pecans are good in this recipe)
4 tsp. baking powder
1 tsp. salt

⅔ cup chilled butter, cut into small pieces
1 cup milk
½ cup maple syrup
Sugar for sprinkling (coarse sugar if you have it, but regular granulated sugar will work also)

Preheat the oven to 425°.

In a large bowl, whisk together the flour, nuts, baking powder, and salt. Cut in the chilled butter until the mixture resembles coarse crumbs. Add the milk and maple syrup and stir to combine; the dough should hold together but be soft. Turn out the dough onto a very lightly floured surface and knead about 5 to 8 times. Roll out the dough into a circle about ½ inch thick. Cut it into 10 to 12 wedges and place them on a greased baking sheet. Sprinkle the tops with a bit of sugar.

Bake for 15 to 18 minutes or until done.

Makes 10 to 12 scones

Orange Cream Scones

....

2 cups all-purpose flour
3 tsp. baking powder
½ tsp. salt
2 T. plus 2 tsp. sugar, divided

¼ cup (½ stick) very cold butter
2 eggs, one of them separated
⅓ cup whipping cream
3 tsp. grated orange peel
¼ tsp. vanilla extract

Preheat the oven to 400°.

In a large mixing bowl, sift together the flour, baking powder, salt, and 2 tablespoons of the sugar. Cut in the butter until the mixture resembles coarse crumbs.

In a separate bowl, separate the yolk of one of the eggs (reserve the egg white to brush the tops of the scones), and stir the yolk together with the other whole egg. Stir in the cream, orange peel, and vanilla.

Make a well in the center of the flour mixture and then pour the egg and cream mixture into the well; stir with a fork just until the dough pulls away from the sides of the bowl.

Sprinkle a clean surface with a small amount of flour. Using your hands, pat the dough into a ball and knead it on the floured surface for about 30 seconds. Divide the dough ball into 2 equal halves. Roll out each half into a circle that is about 1 inch thick and 6 inches in diameter. Cut each circle into 4 pie-shaped wedges and place them about 1 inch apart on an ungreased baking sheet. Brush the tops with the reserved egg white and then sprinkle with the remaining 2 teaspoons of sugar.

Bake for 15 minutes or until done but not too dark. The scones are good plain, but they are even better when topped with marmalade or jam and sweetened whipped cream (page 33).

Makes 8 scones

Pumpkin Biscuits

2½ cups all-purpose flour
¼ cup brown sugar
1 T. baking powder
¾ tsp. salt
¾ tsp. ground cinnamon
¼ tsp. ground ginger

¼ tsp. ground allspice
½ cup shortening
½ cup chopped nuts (walnuts or pecans
    are good choices)
¾ cup canned pumpkin
½ cup milk

Preheat the oven to 450°.

In a large bowl, mix together the dry ingredients, including the spices. Cut in the shortening until the mixture resembles coarse crumbs. Stir in the nuts.

In a small bowl, whisk together the pumpkin and milk until smooth, then add it to the flour mixture and stir with a fork to form a soft dough.

Turn out the dough onto a floured surface and knead for 30 seconds. Roll or pat the dough to a ½-inch thickness and then cut with a biscuit cutter. Place the biscuits on a greased baking sheet and bake for 12 to 14 minutes or until light golden brown and done.

Makes about 10 biscuits

Quick Sourdough Buttermilk Biscuits

2 cups unbleached all-purpose flour
2 tsp. granulated sugar
2 tsp. baking powder
1 tsp. salt

¾ tsp. baking soda
½ cup (1 stick) very cold butter
1 cup active sourdough starter
½ cup buttermilk

Preheat the oven to 425°.

In a large mixing bowl, whisk together the flour, sugar, baking powder, salt, and baking soda. Cut the butter into very small pieces or use the largest holes in a box grater to make coarse shreds. Add the butter to the flour mixture and stir to mix the butter pieces throughout.

In a medium mixing bowl, stir together the starter and the buttermilk. Add the starter mixture to the flour mixture and stir until a soft dough begins to form. (A rubber spatula works well to stir this dough because you can clean the sides of the bowl as you work.) Turn out the dough onto a lightly floured work surface and knead it several times until it comes together.

Roll out or pat the dough to a 1½-inch thickness. Cut the dough into 8 to 10 biscuits, using a 2-inch biscuit cutter or a sharp knife. Place the biscuits onto a baking sheet lined with a silicone baking mat or parchment paper. If the biscuits are spread out, they will have crisper sides. If the sides are touching, you will get softer biscuits.

Bake for 12 to 15 minutes or until done. (If the biscuits are touching, it may take a few more minutes for them to fully bake.)

Makes 8 to 10 biscuits

Quick Sourdough Starter

2 cups warm water (about 110°)
4½ tsp. (2 packets) active dry yeast

2 cups flour
Do not use a metal bowl.

Dissolve the yeast in the water and let it sit until bubbly, about 10 minutes. Stir in the flour. Let it sit at room temperature, covered, at least 2 days before using, stirring occasionally. To store, stir it down, put it into a jar with a lid, and keep it in the refrigerator. When you are ready to use it, remove the starter from the refrigerator and let it sit for 2 hours or until it reaches room temperature.

Savory Potato and Vegetable Scones

2½ to 3 cups all-purpose flour
1 T. plus 1 tsp. baking powder
1½ tsp. salt
⅛ tsp. dried sage
⅛ tsp. dried rosemary
4 oz. cream cheese
½ cup shredded cheddar cheese
1 egg

1 cup cream
1 T. butter
¼ cup finely diced green, red, yellow, and/or orange
  bell peppers (using multiple colors isn't necessary,
  but it makes the scones prettier)
¼ cup finely diced onions
½ large potato, peeled, cooked, and finely diced
⅛ cup thinly sliced or diced fresh mushrooms

Preheat the oven to 400°.

In a medium bowl, mix together the dry ingredients and set aside.

In a large bowl, cream together the cream cheese, shredded cheddar, and egg. Add the cream and mix well.

On medium-low heat, melt the butter in a sauté pan, then add the vegetables and cook until soft, about 4 minutes. Add the cooked vegetables to the bowl with the cream mixture and stir well. Add the dry ingredients and stir by hand until a soft dough forms.

Pat out the dough into a circle that is about 1 inch thick. Place the circle on a cookie sheet that has been buttered or lined with a silicone baking mat. Using a pizza cutter or a knife, cut it into 8 equal wedges, as if you were cutting a pie.

Bake for 20 to 25 minutes or until done. Remove the scones from the baking sheet and set on a wire rack to cool.

Makes 8 scones

Sour Cream Scones with Vanilla Glaze

SCONES
2 cups all-purpose flour
⅓ cup granulated sugar
1½ T. baking powder
1 tsp. baking soda
½ tsp. salt

½ cup (1 stick) very cold
  butter, cut into small cubes
1 egg
½ cup sour cream (use regular
  versus "light" sour cream)
¼ cup heavy cream or half-and-half

GLAZE
1 cup powdered sugar
1 T. milk
½ tsp. vanilla extract
Coarse sugar for sprinkling

Preheat the oven to 400°.

For the scones:

In a large mixing bowl, whisk together the flour, sugar, baking powder, baking soda, and salt. Add the cold butter to the flour mixture and—using two knives or your fingers—quickly work the butter into the flour until there are somewhat smaller pieces. (There will still be small bits of butter scattered in the flour.) Set the mixing bowl into the refrigerator to keep the contents cool.

In a small mixing bowl, whisk the egg to break up the yolk. Next, add the sour cream and heavy cream and whisk to combine.

Remove the flour mixture from the refrigerator and make a well in the center. Add the sour cream mixture and use a fork to mix the ingredients just until the dough comes together but is still shaggy.

Turn out the dough onto parchment paper and pat it into a circle that is about 8 inches in diameter. Cut the circle into 8 pieces as you would cut a pie; place the wedges onto a baking sheet lined with parchment paper.

Refrigerate the wedges on the baking sheet for 15 minutes and then place the scones into the center of the preheated oven. Bake for 15 to 20 minutes or until the scones are a light golden brown on top and the center is baked through. Remove the scones from the baking sheet and cool them on a wire rack.

For the glaze:

In a small mixing bowl, add the powdered sugar, milk, and vanilla and stir together until smooth.

When the scones are cool, drizzle the glaze over the tops and then liberally sprinkle them with coarse sugar.

Enjoy these scones plain or spread with berry jam or lemon curd and a dollop of sweetened whipped cream (page 33).

Makes 8 scones

Yogurt and Sour Cream Biscuits

2 cups all-purpose flour
1 T. sugar
2 tsp. baking powder
½ tsp. baking soda
½ tsp. salt
¼ tsp. oregano

¼ cup (½ stick) very cold butter, cut into
   small pieces
⅔ cup plain yogurt
½ cup milk
¼ cup sour cream
½ cup finely chopped green onions or chives

Preheat the oven to 400°.

Line a baking sheet with parchment paper or a silicone baking mat, or generously grease the baking sheet.

In a large bowl, combine the flour, sugar, baking powder, baking soda, salt, and oregano. Cut in the butter until the mixture resembles coarse crumbs. Add the yogurt, milk, and sour cream and stir gently to form a soft, sticky dough. Stir in the green onions. Using about ¼ cup for each biscuit, drop the dough 2 inches apart onto the prepared baking sheet.

Bake for 15 minutes or until the biscuits are a light golden brown.

Makes about 10 biscuits

Muffins are one of the mainstays in my kitchen recipe collection. They are quick and easy to prepare, and the taste variations are nearly endless. You can make sweet or savory muffins and eat them for breakfast, lunch, dinner, snacks, or dessert. Pretty much any time of the day is muffin time.

Muffins freeze well too, so they make a great last-minute take-along breakfast or snack when heading out the door in the morning. Simply freeze muffins in individual baggies and grab a bag to go—just one example of old-fashioned "fast food."

Some folks use paper cupcake holders to bake their muffins, but I admit to being too frugal for that. Instead, I bake my muffins in well-greased muffin tins, and they slip right out after baking. I remove them from the muffin cups and cool them on wire racks so the bottoms don't get soggy.

Some of our family favorites include Popovers, Blueberry Oatmeal Muffins, and Bacon and Cheddar Cheese Muffins. Whichever recipes you try, I think you'll agree that muffins are a tasty way to satisfy your family's hunger pangs.

To check if a baked good is done, you can insert a toothpick just off-center; if it comes back clean, it's done. Keep in mind, however, that it is fine if there are a few crumbs sticking to the toothpick, but if there is batter clinging to the toothpick, bake for another few minutes and check again.

Apple Pumpkin Muffins with Streusel Topping

MUFFINS
2½ cups all-purpose flour
2 cups sugar
1 T. pumpkin pie spice
1 tsp. baking soda
½ tsp. salt
2 eggs

¾ cup cooked pumpkin
   (or use canned pumpkin)
½ cup cooking oil
2 cups apples, peeled,
   cored, and finely chopped

TOPPING
2 T. flour
¼ cup sugar
½ tsp. cinnamon
2 tsp. butter, softened

Preheat the oven to 350°.

For the muffins:

In a medium bowl, mix together the flour, sugar, pumpkin pie spice, baking soda, and salt. In a large bowl, beat together the eggs, pumpkin, and cooking oil. Add the dry ingredients to the pumpkin mixture and stir until just blended. Don't overmix the batter. Stir in the apple chunks until they are evenly distributed in the batter, then spoon the batter into greased muffin cups until they are about three-quarters full.

For the streusel topping:

Mix together the flour, sugar, and cinnamon; add the butter and mix until combined. Sprinkle the topping evenly over each muffin.

Bake for 30 to 35 minutes or until done. Remove the muffins from the pan and cool them on a wire rack.

Makes about 18 muffins

Bacon and Cheddar Cheese Muffins

2 cups all-purpose flour
2 T. sugar
3 tsp. baking powder
½ tsp. salt
½ cup cooked, crumbled bacon

½ cup shredded cheddar cheese
¼ cup finely diced onions (optional)
1 cup milk
1 egg, beaten
¼ cup (½ stick) butter, melted and cooled
   to lukewarm

Preheat the oven to 425°.

In a large bowl, whisk together the flour, sugar, baking powder, and salt. Add the bacon, cheese, and onions (if using) and mix again. Make a well in the center of the flour mixture.

In a small bowl, mix together the milk, egg, and melted butter. Pour this mixture into the well all at once and stir just until moistened. Do not overmix.

Fill greased muffin cups two-thirds full and bake them for 20 to 25 minutes or until done. Immediately remove the muffins from the pan and place them on a wire rack to cool.

Makes 10 to 12 muffins

Berry Muffins

1¾ cups all-purpose flour
1 cup plus 2 T. sugar, divided
2½ tsp. baking powder
½ tsp. cinnamon
¼ tsp. salt
1 cup milk

¼ cup (½ stick) butter, melted
1 egg, beaten
1 tsp. vanilla extract
1 cup berries, fresh or frozen (blueberries, blackberries, and cranberries all work well)

Preheat the oven to 375°.

In a large bowl, whisk together the flour, 1 cup of the sugar, and the baking powder, cinnamon, and salt.

In another bowl, stir together the milk, butter, egg, and vanilla. Add this to the dry ingredients and stir just until blended. Do not overmix. Fold in the berries.

Fill greased muffin cups three-quarters full. Sprinkle the tops of the muffins with the remaining 2 tablespoons of sugar. Bake for 20 minutes or until done. Remove the muffins from the pan and cool them on a wire rack.

Makes 10 to 12 muffins

Blueberry Oatmeal Muffins

1 cup all-purpose flour
2 tsp. baking powder
½ tsp. salt
½ tsp. cinnamon
½ cup brown sugar
¾ cup rolled oats

1 egg
1 cup milk
¼ cup (½ stick) butter, melted
¾ cup blueberries, fresh or frozen
Sugar or cinnamon sugar for sprinkling

Preheat the oven to 375°.

Whisk together the flour, baking powder, salt, and cinnamon. Add the brown sugar and rolled oats and mix well.

In a large bowl, beat together the egg, milk, and melted butter, then add the dry ingredients and stir just until blended. Do not overmix. Fold in the blueberries.

Fill greased muffin cups two-thirds full and sprinkle sugar (or cinnamon sugar) on top of each muffin. Bake for 20 minutes or until done. Remove the muffins from the pan and cool them on a wire rack.

Makes about 10 muffins

Bran Muffins

1 cup ready-to-eat bran cereal (I use All-Bran)
1 cup milk
2 T. shortening
¼ cup sugar

1 egg, well beaten
1 cup all-purpose flour
3 tsp. baking powder
½ tsp. salt

Preheat the oven to 400°.

In a medium bowl, mix together the bran cereal and milk and let stand for 5 minutes.

In a large bowl, cream together the shortening and sugar. Add the beaten egg and beat until smooth. Add the bran mixture and mix again.

In another bowl whisk together the flour, baking powder, and salt. Add this mixture to the batter and stir just until blended. Do not overmix.

Fill greased muffin cups two-thirds full and bake for 25 minutes or until done. Remove the muffins from the pan and cool them on a wire rack.

Makes about 10 muffins

Cheese Muffins

2 cups all-purpose flour
1 T. sugar
3 tsp. baking powder
½ tsp. salt

¾ cup shredded cheddar cheese
1 cup milk
1 egg, beaten
¼ cup (½ stick) butter, melted

Preheat the oven to 425°.

In a large bowl, whisk together the flour, sugar, baking powder, and salt. Add the cheese and stir to mix.

In a medium bowl, mix together the milk, egg, and melted butter. Make a well in the center of the flour mixture and pour the liquid mixture into the well all at once, then stir just until moistened. Do not overmix.

Fill greased muffin cups two-thirds full and bake for 20 to 25 minutes or until done. Remove the muffins from the pan and cool them on a wire rack.

Makes 10 to 12 muffins

Most recipes can be doubled with no alterations to the method.

Chocolate Chip Muffins

1½ cups all-purpose flour
½ cup sugar
2 tsp. baking powder
½ tsp. salt

1 egg
½ cup milk
¼ cup cooking oil
¾ cup chocolate chips

Preheat the oven to 400°.

In a large bowl, whisk together the flour, sugar, baking powder, and salt.

In another bowl, beat the egg and then add it to the flour mixture along with the milk and cooking oil. Stir just until blended. Don't overmix. Gently fold in the chocolate chips.

Fill greased muffins cups about two-thirds full. Bake for 20 to 25 minutes or until done. Remove the muffins from the pan and cool them on a wire rack.

Makes about 10 muffins

Cornmeal Muffins

....

1 cup all-purpose flour	½ tsp. salt
1 cup cornmeal	1 cup milk
3 T. sugar	1 egg, beaten
3 tsp. baking powder	¼ cup (½ stick) butter, melted

Preheat the oven to 425°.

In a large bowl, whisk together the flour, cornmeal, sugar, baking powder, and salt.

In a medium bowl, mix together the milk, egg, and melted butter. Make a well in the center of the flour mixture and then add the liquid mixture into the well all at once. Stir just until moistened. Do not overmix.

Fill greased muffin cups two-thirds full and bake for 20 to 25 minutes or until done. Remove the muffins from the pan and cool them on a wire rack.

Makes about 8 muffins

Four-Week Refrigerator Bran Muffins

....

6 cups ready-to-eat bran cereal, divided	5 cups all-purpose flour
2 cups boiling water	5 tsp. baking soda
1 cup shortening or butter, room temperature	1 tsp. salt
1½ cups sugar	Raisins, dates, other dried fruit, or nuts,
4 eggs	coarsely chopped (optional)
1 quart buttermilk	

To make the batter:

Place 2 cups of the bran cereal into a medium bowl and pour in the boiling water. Set aside to cool. Meanwhile, in a very large bowl, cream together the shortening or butter, sugar, and eggs. Add the buttermilk and the cooled cereal mixture.

In a large bowl, whisk together the flour, baking soda, and salt and add to the creamed mixture. Stir until the flour is blended. Fold in the remaining 4 cups of dry bran cereal and the dried fruit or nuts, if using.

Store the batter in a covered container in the refrigerator for up to 4 weeks.

To use:

When you are ready to bake the muffins, preheat the oven to 400° and fill well-greased muffin cups two-thirds full. Bake the muffins for 20 minutes or until done. Remove the muffins from the pan and cool them on a wire rack.

Makes more than a gallon of batter, but it goes fast because it's so convenient. It should make a little more than 3 dozen muffins.

Ginger Muffins

¼ cup shortening
¼ cup sugar
1 egg
½ cup molasses
1½ cups all-purpose flour
¾ tsp. baking soda

¼ tsp. salt
½ tsp. cinnamon
½ tsp. ground ginger
¼ tsp. ground cloves
¼ cup wheat or oat bran
½ cup buttermilk

Preheat the oven to 375°.

In a large bowl, cream together the shortening and sugar. Beat in the egg and then the molasses.

In another large bowl, whisk together the flour, baking soda, salt, cinnamon, ginger, cloves, and bran. Stir the flour mixture into the molasses mixture and then gradually add the buttermilk, beating until smooth.

Fill greased muffin cups two-thirds full and bake for 20 to 25 minutes or until done. Remove the muffins from the pan and cool them on a wire rack.

Makes about 10 muffins

Honey Muffins

2 cups all-purpose flour
½ cup sugar
3 tsp. baking powder
½ tsp. salt

1 egg
1 cup milk
¼ cup (½ stick) butter, melted
¼ cup honey

Preheat the oven to 400°.

In a large bowl, mix together the flour, sugar, baking powder, and salt.

In a small bowl, mix together the egg, milk, butter, and honey. Stir this mixture into the flour mixture just until moistened. Don't overmix.

Fill greased muffin cups about two-thirds full and bake for 15 to 18 minutes or until done. Let the pan cool for 5 minutes and then remove the muffins to cool on a wire rack. These muffins, however, are best eaten warm.

Makes about 8 muffins

WHEN MEASURING STICKY INGREDIENTS, such as honey, molasses, corn syrup, or maple syrup, lightly coat your measuring tool with oil, and the sticky ingredients will pour right out.

Jam Muffins

2 cups all-purpose flour	1 cup milk
3 T. sugar	1 egg, beaten
3 tsp. baking powder	¼ cup (½ stick) butter, melted
½ tsp. salt	6 tsp. jam, more or less (any flavor of jam will do)

Preheat the oven to 425°.

In a large bowl, whisk together the flour, sugar, baking powder, and salt.

In a medium bowl, mix together the milk, egg, and melted butter. Make a well in the center of the flour mixture and then add the liquid mixture into the well all at once. Stir just until moistened. Do not overmix.

Fill greased muffin cups two-thirds full; add ½ teaspoon jam (or a bit more if you desire) to the top of each muffin, and bake for 20 to 25 minutes or until done. Remove the muffins from the pan and cool them on a wire rack.

Makes about 10 muffins

Lemon Muffins

2 cups all-purpose flour	2 T. sugar
3 tsp. baking powder	1⅓ cups milk
½ tsp. salt	¼ cup cooking oil
1 box instant lemon pudding mix	Powdered sugar for sprinkling (optional)

Preheat the oven to 425°.

In a large bowl, whisk together the flour, baking powder, salt, pudding mix, and sugar. In another bowl, mix together the milk and cooking oil and pour it into the flour mixture, stirring just until blended. Do not overmix.

Fill greased muffin cups two-thirds full and bake for 20 to 25 minutes or until done. Remove the muffins from the oven and place them on a wire rack to cool. Sprinkle them with powdered sugar if desired.

Makes about 8 muffins

The experts recommend using unsalted butter in baked goods. Now, I might be a baking cretin, but I never keep unsalted butter around, and I've been baking goodies without the use of unsalted butter for many years without so much as a peep from anyone.

Maple Crumb Muffins

MUFFINS

2 cups all-purpose flour
½ cup brown sugar
2 tsp. baking powder
½ tsp. salt
¾ cup milk
½ cup (1 stick) butter, melted
½ cup maple syrup

¼ cup sour cream
1 egg
½ tsp. vanilla extract

TOPPING

3 T. all-purpose flour
3 T. sugar
2 T. finely chopped walnuts
  or pecans
½ tsp. cinnamon
2 T. (¼ stick) very cold butter,
  cubed

Preheat the oven to 400°.

For the muffins:

In a large bowl, mix together the flour, brown sugar, baking powder, and salt.

In another bowl, combine the milk, melted butter, maple syrup, sour cream, egg, and vanilla. Stir the wet ingredients into the flour mixture just until moistened. Don't overmix. Fill greased muffin cups about two-thirds full.

For the crumb topping:

Mix together the flour, sugar, nuts, and cinnamon; cut in the butter until the mixture resembles coarse crumbs. Sprinkle the crumb topping over the tops of the muffin batter.

Bake for 16 to 20 minutes until done. Leave the muffins in the pan for 5 minutes to cool before removing them to a wire rack to cool completely.

Makes about 10 muffins

Oatmeal, Apple, and Raisin Muffins

1 egg
¾ cup milk
½ cup cooking oil
1 cup uncooked rolled oats
1 cup chopped apples
1 cup raisins

1 cup all-purpose flour
⅓ cup sugar
3 tsp. baking powder
2 tsp. cinnamon
1 tsp. salt
1 tsp. nutmeg

Preheat the oven to 400°.

In a large bowl, beat the egg; add the milk and oil and stir until mixed. Add the remaining ingredients and stir just until blended. Do not overmix. Fill greased muffin cups about three-quarters full.

Bake for 15 to 20 minutes or until done. Remove the muffins from the pan and cool them on a wire rack.

Makes 12 muffins

Orange Muffins

2 cups all-purpose flour
½ cup sugar
3 T. baking powder
1 T. grated orange peel
½ tsp. salt

¾ cup milk
¼ cup (½ stick) butter, melted
¼ cup orange juice
1 egg, beaten

Preheat the oven to 425°.

In a large bowl, whisk together the flour, sugar, baking powder, orange peel, and salt.

In a medium bowl, mix together the milk, butter, orange juice, and egg.

Make a well in the center of the flour mixture and then add the liquid mixture all at once into the well. Stir just until moistened. Do not overmix.

Fill greased muffin cups two-thirds full and bake for 20 to 25 minutes or until done. Remove the muffins from the pan and cool on a wire rack.

Makes 8 muffins

Popovers

1 cup flour
¼ tsp. salt (I usually go a little heavy on the salt)
1 tsp. sugar (optional—we don't use sugar because we eat our popovers as a savory side to our meal, but cook's choice)

1 T. butter, melted and cooled
1 cup milk
2 eggs

Preheat the oven to 375°.

Grease or butter 10 (½-cup) custard cups or muffin cups.

In a mixing bowl, combine the flour, salt, and sugar (if you're using it) and mix thoroughly. Add the butter, milk, and eggs; beat until the batter is very smooth, about 2½ minutes, remembering to scrape the sides often.

Fill the prepared custard cups or muffin cups about halfway and bake them on the center rack of your oven for 50 to 55 minutes.

Makes 10 popovers

Note: *Like a soufflé, popovers wait for no one. When you take them from the oven to the table, they will begin to deflate as they cool. So have everyone gathered and ready when they are done.*

Raisin Muffins

....

2 cups all-purpose flour
3 T. sugar
3 tsp. baking powder
½ tsp. salt

½ to ¾ cup raisins
1 cup milk
1 egg, beaten
¼ cup (½ stick) butter, melted

Preheat the oven to 425°.

In a large bowl, whisk together the flour, sugar, baking powder, and salt, then stir in the raisins.

In a medium bowl, mix together the milk, egg, and melted butter. Make a well in the center of the flour mixture and then add the liquid mixture into the well all at once. Stir just until moistened. Do not overmix.

Fill the greased muffin cups two-thirds full and bake for 20 to 25 minutes or until done. Remove the muffins from the pan and cool them on a wire rack.

Makes about 10 muffins

Rhubarb Muffins

....

MUFFINS
1½ cups all-purpose flour
1 cup whole wheat flour
1 tsp. baking soda
1 tsp. baking powder
½ tsp. salt
1 cup buttermilk, or plain yogurt

¾ cup brown sugar
½ cup cooking oil
1 egg, beaten
2 tsp. vanilla extract
1½ cups rhubarb, diced

TOPPING
¼ cup sugar
1 T. butter, melted
1 tsp. cinnamon
1 tsp. flour

Preheat the oven to 375°.

For the muffins:

In a medium bowl, whisk together the all-purpose flour, whole wheat flour, baking soda, baking powder, and salt. In a large bowl, combine the buttermilk (or yogurt), brown sugar, cooking oil, egg, and vanilla. Add the flour mixture to the wet ingredients and stir to combine. Fold in the rhubarb. Fill greased muffin cups two-thirds full with batter.

For the topping:

Mix together the sugar, melted butter, cinnamon, and flour, then sprinkle the topping over the muffin batter.

Bake the muffins for 20 minutes or until done. Remove them from the pan and cool them on a wire rack.

Makes about 12 muffins

Summer Peach Muffins

1 cup fresh peaches, peeled and chopped	3 tsp. baking powder
1 tsp. lemon juice	1 cup milk
⅔ cup sugar	1 egg
½ tsp. salt	¼ cup (½ stick) butter, melted
¼ tsp. cinnamon	2 cups all-purpose flour

Preheat the oven to 375°.

In a small bowl, sprinkle the peach chunks with the lemon juice, mix to coat, and then set aside.

In a large bowl, mix together the sugar, salt, cinnamon, and baking powder. Add the milk, egg, and butter and mix well. Add the flour and mix again, being careful to not overmix. Fold in the fruit and then fill greased muffin cups two-thirds full.

Bake for 20 minutes or until done. Remove the muffins from the pan and cool them on a wire rack.

Makes about 8 muffins

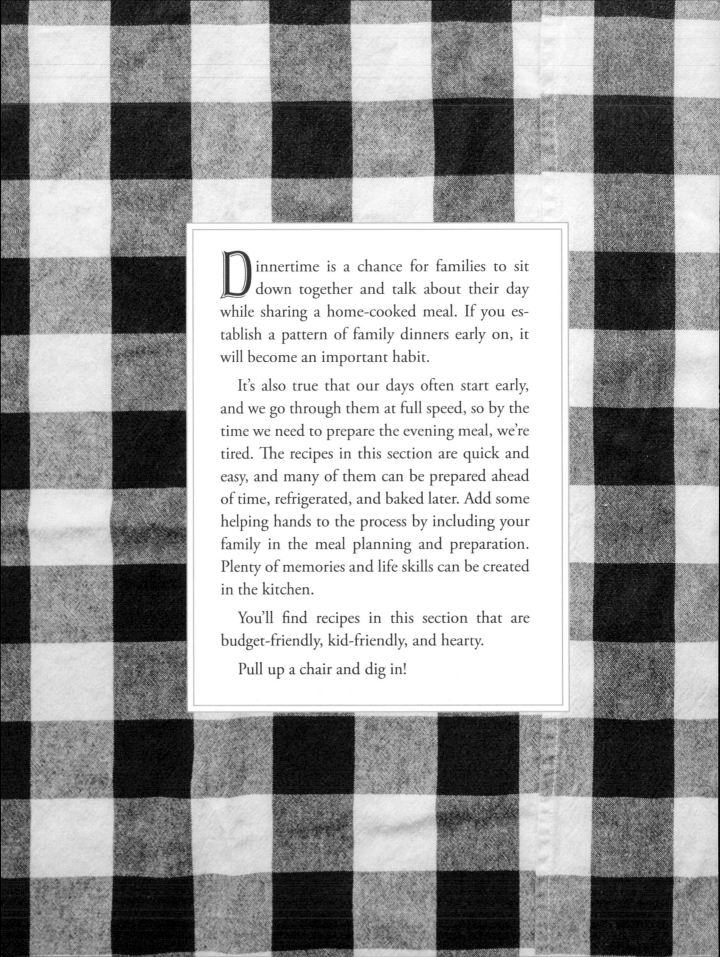

Dinnertime is a chance for families to sit down together and talk about their day while sharing a home-cooked meal. If you establish a pattern of family dinners early on, it will become an important habit.

It's also true that our days often start early, and we go through them at full speed, so by the time we need to prepare the evening meal, we're tired. The recipes in this section are quick and easy, and many of them can be prepared ahead of time, refrigerated, and baked later. Add some helping hands to the process by including your family in the meal planning and preparation. Plenty of memories and life skills can be created in the kitchen.

You'll find recipes in this section that are budget-friendly, kid-friendly, and hearty.

Pull up a chair and dig in!

MAIN DISHES
AND
CASSEROLES

Beef and Biscuit Casserole

Basic biscuit dough, cut into circles but
   unbaked (see Basic Biscuits, page 29)
1½ lbs. ground beef
½ cup onion, chopped
4 oz. cream cheese

¼ cup milk
1 (10½ oz.) can cream of mushroom soup
1 tsp. salt
½ cup catsup

Preheat the oven to 375°.

Brown the ground beef and onion; drain. Mix the cooked meat with the cream cheese, milk, cream of mushroom soup, salt, and catsup. Spread the mixture into a lightly buttered 9 x 9-inch or 9 x 11-inch baking dish and bake for 15 minutes. Then place the unbaked biscuits on top, leaving room between them to rise while baking. Return the dish to the oven and bake for about 20 minutes more or until the biscuits are done and golden on top.

Serves 6

Cabbage Casserole with Ground Beef

2 small heads cabbage, chopped
1 lb. ground beef
½ cup onion, chopped
1 pint sour cream

1 large can tomato juice (about 1 quart)
1 cup cheddar cheese, shredded
1 tsp. salt
½ tsp. pepper

Preheat the oven to 400°.

In a large pot, boil the chopped cabbage until it is slightly wilted; drain and set aside. In a skillet, brown the ground beef and onion, then drain off the fat.

In a large bowl, mix together the cabbage, meat, and remaining ingredients, and pour it all into a 9 x 13-inch baking dish, and bake for 45 minutes. (Check the casserole while it is baking and turn down the oven temperature if your casserole is browning too quickly.)

Serves 6 to 8

Tip: *If you like a bit of extra crunch from cabbage, you can forego the pre-boiling and save time. I have made this casserole countless times and rarely take the time to boil the cabbage. Instead, I head straight to the instruction to brown the meat and onion, and I add the cabbage along with everything else when mixing.*

Chicken Fajitas

2 T. olive oil
3 boneless skinless chicken breasts (about 1 lb.),
  cut into thin slices
1 large onion, thinly sliced
1 green bell pepper, seeded, cut in half lengthwise,
  and thinly sliced
1 orange or yellow bell pepper, seeded, cut in
  half lengthwise, and thinly sliced
8 oz. mushrooms, sliced (optional)
2 large tomatoes, cut in large, bite-size pieces

¼ cup water, divided
1 T. chili powder (more or less, to taste)
½ tsp. garlic powder
½ tsp. cumin
½ tsp. dried oregano
2 T. fresh cilantro, minced
Salt and pepper to taste
1 T. lemon or lime juice
Flour or corn tortillas
Shredded cheddar cheese and sour cream (optional)

In a large skillet, cook the chicken in the olive oil on medium heat until lightly browned.

Add the vegetables, turn the heat to medium-high, and continue to cook for 5 minutes, stirring often. Add ⅛ cup water, turn the heat down to medium, cover the skillet, and allow the chicken and vegetables to continue cooking for 5 to 10 minutes or until the vegetables are somewhat tender and the chicken is cooked completely. You may need to add a small amount of extra water during this cooking phase if it starts to get too dry.

Remove the lid, turn the heat up a bit, and then add the chili powder, garlic powder, cumin, oregano, cilantro, salt, pepper, lemon juice, and the remaining ⅛ cup of water. Continue cooking, uncovered, until the liquid has mostly evaporated, about another 3 minutes. Taste and adjust the seasonings as desired.

Serve the fajitas rolled in tortillas, with cheese and sour cream if desired.

Serves 6 to 8

If a recipe calls for thinly sliced meat (such as when making fajitas or stir fry), use partially frozen meat—you'll get a thinner cut. If your meat is completely defrosted, place it in the freezer for about 20 minutes and then cut it against the grain.

Chicken un Kraut

1 (3 to 4 lb.) roasting chicken, or you can use
  a young duck if you prefer
1 onion, quartered

2 quarts sauerkraut
1 cup water
2 T. sugar

Preheat the oven to 450°.

Place the chicken in a roasting pan and sprinkle with salt and pepper. Stuff the cavity with the onion quarters. Add the sauerkraut and water around the chicken in the bottom of the roasting pan. Sprinkle sugar over the sauerkraut. Cover and place the chicken in the oven, reducing the heat to 375°. Bake until the chicken is cooked through and tender and juices run clear, about 1½ hours.

Serves 5 to 6

Cornflake Baked Chicken

⅓ cup mayonnaise
½ tsp. salt
½ tsp. garlic salt

½ tsp. dried rosemary
1 (3 to 3½ lb.) frying chicken, cut into pieces
1½ cups crushed cornflakes

Preheat the oven to 350°.

In a bowl, mix together the mayonnaise, salt, garlic salt, and rosemary. Place the crushed corn-flakes in a shallow dish, such as a pie pan. Brush the pieces of chicken with the mayonnaise mixture and then roll them in the cornflakes.

Place the chicken, skin side up, in a lightly greased baking pan; don't crowd the pieces. Bake the chicken uncovered for 1 hour or until all chicken pieces are thoroughly cooked.

I've used this recipe with boneless, skinless chicken breasts with great success, although I reduce the bake time by about 20 minutes. How long you bake the chicken is contingent upon the size of the individual pieces.

Serves 5

Cottage Pie

2 T. butter
2 cups leftover cooked meat (any kind), diced
3 T. flour

1 can vegetable soup plus enough water to
   make a total of 2 cups
Leftover mashed potatoes (or make a fresh batch,
   enough to cover your pie)

Preheat the oven to 375°.

In a medium saucepan over medium heat, melt the butter and add the diced meat; cook, stirring, until the meat is hot. Add the flour and stir until well blended to make a roux, then pour in the soup mixture and cook, stirring constantly, until the mixture has thickened into a runny gravy.

Turn out the complete contents of the skillet into a 9 x 9-inch baking dish. Top the meat mixture with a thick layer of mashed potatoes. Bake for about 20 minutes or until the potatoes are lightly browned on top.

Serves 5

Note: *I often make this dish using ground beef that I cook fresh. Just omit the butter in this recipe when cooking the meat, and do not drain off the fat after browning the meat, but use the fat to make the gravy. This will give a nice flavor to the finished dish. Add butter to the fat only if needed to equal 2 tablespoons. Add the flour and proceed as directed with the soup and other ingredients. Also, I usu-ally use a pint jar of my home-canned vegetable soup in place of a store-bought can of soup. Really, this is the sort of recipe that doesn't take careful measuring. Just throw what you have on hand into the pot and top it with mashed potatoes that have been made with rich milk and plenty of butter.*

Creamy Baked Chicken

CHICKEN	SAUCE	
2 lbs. (6 to 8 pieces) bone-in chicken thighs	2 T. butter	¼ cup grated Parmesan cheese
	4 cloves garlic, minced	Salt and pepper to taste
1 T. Italian seasoning	1 tsp. Italian seasoning	
½ tsp. salt	2 T. all-purpose flour	
¼ tsp. pepper	1 cup chicken broth or water	
2 T. butter	½ cup heavy cream or half-and-half	

Preheat the oven to 375°.

For the chicken:

Season the chicken pieces with the Italian seasoning, salt, and pepper.

Melt the butter in a large, oven-proof skillet over medium heat. Add the chicken pieces, skin-side down, and brown both sides until golden brown, about 2 minutes on each side. Remove the chicken from the skillet and set it aside for now.

For the cream sauce:

Make sure all ingredients are measured out and ready to go before you start to make the cream sauce, since this is a very hands-on process.

Melt the butter in the same skillet over medium heat. Add the garlic and cook, whisking, until it is fragrant but not browned, about 2 minutes. Continuing to whisk constantly, add the Italian seasoning and flour. Next, whisk in the chicken broth. When the broth has been fully incorporated, whisk in the cream and Parmesan cheese, stirring for another minute or two until the sauce is slightly thickened. Turn off the heat but keep the skillet on the stove. Season with salt and pepper.

Place the browned chicken pieces back into the skillet, keeping the tops of the chicken pieces above the cream sauce so the skin crisps during baking. Place the skillet in the oven and bake for about 35 minutes or until the chicken is cooked through.

Serves 4 to 6

The USDA advises that you can refreeze meat if it was thawed in the refrigerator. Note that if you do refreeze the meat, there will probably be a loss of quality, but it's totally safe to cook and eat later. But never refreeze foods that have been left outside the refrigerator for longer than two hours.

Ground Beef Dressing Casserole

1 lb. ground beef
1 medium onion, chopped
1 (10½ oz.) can cream of chicken soup
1 (10½ oz.) can cream of celery or cream of
    mushroom soup

2 soup cans (21 oz. total) water or chicken broth
5 cups seasoned bread cubes or croutons
    (the kind you use in your turkey dressing)

Preheat the oven to 350°.

In a large pot over medium heat, brown the ground beef and onion; remove from the heat and drain off the fat. Add the soups to the pot, fill each soup can with water, and then pour all the water in as well. Alternately, you can use chicken broth instead of water. Thoroughly combine the meat and the liquids.

Butter a large baking dish and spread the bread cubes evenly in the dish. Pour the soup and meat mixture evenly over the top of the bread cubes, adding a bit more water if you like your dressing to be more moist.

Bake for 25 minutes or until the casserole is bubbly and lightly browned on top.

Serves 5

Halibut Florentine

3 T. butter, divided
2 T. flour
1 cup milk
1 lb. halibut fillets (alternatively, you could
    use sole, bass, or tilapia fillets)
1 cup water

4 T. lemon juice
1¼ cups chopped spinach, cooked, drained,
    and squeezed dry
¾ cup sharp cheddar cheese, shredded and divided
3 green onions, chopped
Salt and pepper to taste

Preheat the oven to 400°.

In a small saucepan over medium-low heat, melt 2 tablespoons of butter. Whisk in the flour and then add the milk, continuing to whisk constantly. Raise the heat to medium and continue stirring until the mixture thickens and begins to boil. Remove the white sauce from the heat and add salt and pepper to taste.

Place the halibut fillets in a shallow saucepan. Add the water and lemon juice, cover, and simmer for 5 minutes. Remove the fish with a slotted spoon and place the fillets in a lightly buttered baking dish. With the broth still in the saucepan and the cover removed, raise the heat to a gentle boil, until the broth is reduced to two thirds the original volume. Stir in the white sauce, spinach, ¼ cup of the cheese, and the green onions. Stir constantly until the sauce comes to a gentle simmer and then quickly remove it from the heat. Sprinkle the fillets with salt and pepper. Pour the sauce over the halibut and sprinkle with the remaining cheese. Dot the fish with the remaining tablespoon of butter and bake until golden brown, about 8 to 10 minutes.

Serves 4

Ham and Egg Noodle Bake

EGG NOODLES

1 cup flour, plus more for kneading
½ tsp. salt
2 eggs, beaten

THE BAKE

2 cups cooked egg noodles
1½ cups cooked ham, diced
3 eggs, beaten
1½ cups milk
Salt and pepper to taste

For the noodles:

In a mixing bowl, stir together the flour and salt. Make a well in the middle and add the eggs. Using a fork, start mixing the flour into the eggs and keep incorporating more of the flour into the dough until it forms a ball; it will be sticky but should hold together.

Turn out the dough ball onto a floured surface and use your hands to keep working in the flour, kneading as you go, and adding more flour if needed. You want the dough to be smooth and no longer sticky, but not too dry. Wrap the dough in plastic wrap and chill in the refrigerator for 30 minutes. (Sometimes when I am in a hurry, I don't chill my dough, and I don't seem to have any problems with skipping the chilling step.)

Remove the chilled dough, place it back on the floured work surface, and cut it into two even pieces. Working with one half at a time and keeping the other half wrapped, roll out the dough as thin as you desire, and then cut the dough into noodles. Let the noodles sit on a drying rack for about 30 minutes or so before cooking.

To cook the noodles, bring a large pot of salted water to a good boil. Drop in the noodles and stir occasionally until they are done cooking, then drain them in a colander. The boiling time will vary, but you can figure somewhere between 5 and 10 minutes, depending on the thickness of the noodles.

For the bake:

Preheat the oven to 350°.

Heavily grease a 9 x 13-inch baking dish. Spread two cups of cooked noodles in the dish, and then scatter the ham on top of the noodles.

Beat together the eggs, milk, salt, and pepper, then pour the sauce over the noodles and ham and bake for 30 minutes.

Serves 4

Ham Loaf

3 T. butter	½ cup bread crumbs
5 T. brown sugar	¼ cup milk
3 slices pineapple	2 eggs, slightly beaten
1½ lbs. cooked ground ham	Salt and pepper to taste

Preheat the oven to 375°.

In the loaf pan you plan to use, melt the butter; add the brown sugar and stir until the sugar is dissolved. Lay the pineapple slices evenly across the bottom of the pan.

Using your hands, mix together the ham, bread crumbs, milk, eggs, salt, and pepper. Spread the meat mixture over the pineapple slices and bake for 1 hour. To serve, turn out the ham loaf onto a serving platter so the pineapple is right side up.

Serves 6

Tip: *You might wonder where to get cooked ground ham, but there's an easy way to accomplish this at home if you don't have a meat grinder. You can easily find 1-lb. cans of cooked ham; buy two, and either lavishly use it all in this recipe (if your loaf pan is big enough) or save out half of one can for something else, such as scrambled eggs and diced ham for breakfast. When you open the can of ham, simply turn it out onto a cutting board and smash the ham with a meat tenderizer or your hands. Voilà! You're ready to go.*

Huntington Casserole

4 T. butter	2 cups uncooked egg noodles (page 72)
4 T. flour	1 cup cheddar cheese, shredded
1 cup milk	Cracker crumbs, bread crumbs, or crushed
2 cups chicken broth	potato chips
2 cups cooked, diced chicken	

Preheat the oven to 350° and butter or grease a 9 x 9-inch casserole dish.

In a large saucepan, melt the butter and then whisk the flour into the butter to form a roux. Add the milk and then the broth in a steady stream, whisking constantly to make a white sauce. Keep whisking and cooking until the sauce thickens, then remove the pan from the heat.

Gently stir the chicken, egg noodles, and cheddar cheese into the white sauce. Do not overmix, to avoid shredding the chicken. Spoon the mixture into the prepared dish and top with the cracker crumbs. Bake for 35 to 45 minutes or until the casserole is bubbly and cooked through.

Serves 5

Leftover Meat Pie

This recipe is a great way to use up your leftover gravy, leftover meat, and leftover vegetables from other meals. I've included a recipe for fresh gravy you can use if needed.

GRAVY
¼ cup broth or pan drippings
3 T. flour
1 cup milk

PIE
Double crust pie shell, unbaked
 (see Mama's Pie Crust, page 191)
1½ cups leftover meat, more or less,
 cut into small cubes
½ cup mixed vegetables, cooked and diced, such
 as potatoes, carrots, corn, onions, or peas
1 cup gravy
Salt and pepper to taste

For the gravy:

After roasting meat, the pan drippings (all the lovely broth and fat left behind in the pan) make a delicious gravy. You can also use broth. Simply heat the broth or drippings in a saucepan over medium heat, then gradually add the flour, stirring constantly, to form a roux. Once the roux is smooth, gradually add the milk and continue to cook, stirring constantly, until the sauce thickens.

If you already have prepared gravy, reheat it in a saucepan over medium heat.

For the meat pie:

Preheat the oven to 425°.

Place one unbaked pie crust shell in a pie pan.

Mix the meat and vegetables into the warm gravy, adding salt and pepper to taste. Pour the meat mixture into the unbaked pie crust. Place the top crust over the filling, crimp the edges of the two crusts together, and make several small slashes across the top to vent.

Bake for 25 minutes or until the crust is golden and the meat filling is bubbling.

Serves 6

Don't throw out leftover broth or gravy. Freeze it in ice cube trays, and when it's completely frozen, place the cubes in a freezer bag to store until needed to flavor soups, stews, or casseroles.

Old-Fashioned Beef Pot Pie

FILLING

2 lbs. beef stew meat, cubed
6 potatoes, chopped or thinly sliced
2 onions, chopped or thinly sliced
¼ cup fresh parsley, chopped fine
   (or use a scant ⅛ cup dried)
Salt and pepper to taste

DOUGH

2 cups flour, plus more for rolling
Pinch of salt
1 egg, beaten

For the dough:

In a medium mixing bowl, add a pinch of salt to the flour. Make a well in the flour and add the egg. Stir or use your hands to make a stiff dough, adding more flour if needed. On a floured surface, roll out the dough as thin as possible and then cut it into 2-inch squares.

For the filling:

In a large pot, add the beef cubes and enough water to cover. Season with a bit of salt and pepper and boil the beef for an hour or two or until it is tender. Add more water if necessary to keep the meat covered—don't let it boil dry. When the meat is tender, remove it from the broth and set the meat aside for now, leaving the broth in the pot.

Meanwhile, peel and cut the potatoes and onions and set them aside as well.

To assemble the pot pie:

Divide your filling ingredients into two even sets. Into the hot broth in the pot, make layers of potatoes, onions, parsley, and pot pie squares. Repeat the layers, ending with pot pie dough squares on top. (You will add the meat at the end.)

Cover the pot and simmer on medium-low for 20 minutes; don't lift the cover! After the pot pie is cooked, return the meat to the pot, cover, and cook it on low just until the meat is heated through.

Many of us think *meat pie* when we hear the words *pot pie*. This version of pot pie doesn't use a crust and is more like a meat and noodle squares dish. It is—to my way of thinking, at least—more traditional.

I sometimes add Kitchen Bouquet or a couple of bouillon cubes for a richer taste.

Serves 6 to 8

It's cheaper to buy meat in bulk than in individual pieces. So if you have freezer space, investigate buying a quarter or half of beef or pork and potentially save hundreds of dollars.

One-Dish Meal

1 (3 to 4 lb.) chicken, cut into pieces
Flour, to coat the chicken
Salt and pepper to taste
1 to 2 T. cooking oil

5 potatoes, peeled and thickly sliced
1 bunch green onions, sliced
1 (10½ oz.) can cream of mushroom soup
1 soup can water

Roll chicken pieces in flour seasoned with salt and pepper. In a heavy-bottomed pot that can hold all the pieces at once, heat the oil over medium heat. Use enough oil to cover the bottom of the pan in a very thin layer so the pieces don't stick. Add the chicken to the pot and brown the meat well on all sides.

Layer the potatoes over the chicken, and then place the green onions on top of the potatoes.

In a small bowl, mix together the soup and water and pour the liquid over the top of the chicken and vegetables. Bring the soup to a simmer, then turn the heat to low and cover the pot, continuing to simmer for about 20 to 30 minutes or until the chicken is cooked through and the potatoes are tender.

You can serve this meal on plates, but large, shallow pasta bowls work well also.

Serves 6 to 8

Poor Man's Steak

1 lb. ground beef
1 cup cracker crumbs
1 cup milk
1 tsp. salt
¼ tsp. pepper

1 small onion, chopped (optional)
Flour, to coat
Cooking oil or spray
1 (10½ oz.) can cream of mushroom soup
½ soup can water

In a large bowl, mix together all the ingredients except the flour, soup, and water. Press the meat mixture into a cookie sheet or loaf pan, cover, and refrigerate at least 8 hours or overnight.

When ready to bake, cut the meat into slices or rectangles of about 3 x 4 inches. Dredge each slice in flour. Heat a frying pan over medium heat with a bit of oil or cooking spray to prevent the meat from sticking, and brown the meat slices, flipping once to brown each side.

Lay the pieces in a roasting pan close together in one layer. In a small bowl, mix together the soup and water and spread the liquid over the meat. Bake the "steaks" at 350° for 1 hour.

Serves 6

Pot Roast with Carrots and Potatoes

1 T. oil
1 (3 to 4 lb.) boneless chuck or round roast
4 to 6 potatoes, peeled and quartered
6 to 8 carrots, peeled and quartered

Cornstarch
Water
Salt and pepper to taste

In a large stockpot or Dutch oven, heat the oil over medium heat; sprinkle the roast with salt and pepper and then place it in the pot and brown all sides. Fill the pot with enough water to barely cover the meat. Bring the water to a boil and then reduce the heat to low, cover the pot, and simmer for about 3 hours. Add the potatoes and carrots, making sure they are submerged in the cooking liquid. (You may need to add a bit more water.) Once again bring the contents to a boil and then reduce the heat, cover the pot, and cook until the potatoes and carrots are tender, about another half hour.

Using a big slotted spoon, remove the meat, potatoes, and carrots from the pot. Keeping them separate, place them in heatproof dishes and set them aside to keep warm. (I usually turn my oven on for a few minutes just to get the inside a bit warm and then turn off the heat and set my meat and veggies in the warm oven.)

For the gravy:

Keep the broth simmering in the Dutch oven. Estimate how many cups of broth you have in your pot, and for every cup of broth measure out 1 tablespoon of cornstarch and 1 tablespoon of water. Make a cornstarch slurry by mixing the cornstarch and water in a pourable mixing bowl or large liquid measuring cup. (I usually use a bit more water than cornstarch so it's a thinner slurry, but that's not necessary.) Slowly pour the slurry into the simmering broth, stirring constantly so the cornstarch doesn't clump. Continue stirring until the broth begins to bubble and thicken and the gravy becomes a bit clearer looking. Taste the gravy and add salt and pepper if needed.

To serve, put the meat, carrots, and potatoes on individual plates and either pour gravy over everything or bring the gravy to the table and let everyone pour their own.

Serves 6

Roasted Herbed Chicken

1 (3 lb.) whole chicken, giblets removed
1 apple, skinned, quartered, and cored
1 small onion (or half of a large onion), quartered
1 quart chicken broth or water, divided
2 tsp. dried parsley
1 tsp. dried sage
1 tsp. dried rosemary
1 tsp. dried thyme
½ tsp. dried marjoram
½ tsp. dried oregano
½ tsp. dried garlic, granulated or minced
Salt and pepper to taste
3 cups hot cooked rice

Preheat the oven to 350°.

Rinse the chicken and place the apple and onion pieces inside the cavity. Fill as well as you can—you may have leftover pieces that don't quite fit inside. Place the chicken into a deep-sided roasting pan. (I use a cast-iron Dutch oven.) Pour about 2 cups of the broth into the roasting pan and then sprinkle the herbs all over the chicken and into the broth. Cover the roasting pan and place it in the oven.

Roast the chicken until done, about 1½ to 2 hours, removing the lid after about 45 minutes or so. Periodically spoon the broth over the chicken and add more broth as necessary. You want there to be plenty of broth at the end of the baking period.

To serve, slice the chicken. Place a portion of the hot cooked rice onto plates that have sides or into pasta or soup bowls. Add slices of chicken and then ladle the broth over the chicken and rice.

Serves 6

Note: *In our family we call this Green Chicken, it is a family favorite.*

Simple Meat Loaf

2½ lb. ground beef
2½ cups bread crumbs
1 cup cheese, coarsely shredded or finely cubed
¼ cup green pepper, diced
¼ cup onion, diced
2 eggs
1 cup catsup, divided
Salt and pepper to taste

In a large bowl and using your fingers, mix together all ingredients, reserving ½ cup catsup for the top. Form the meat into two loaves and put them in loaf pans. Spread the remaining catsup evenly over the tops of the loaves and bake them at 350° for 1 hour and 15 minutes or until done.

Serves 12

Zucchini Boats

3 zucchini, about 8 inches long
1 lb. ground beef
1 medium onion, chopped
½ cup sliced mushrooms

1 cup bell pepper, chopped (use different colors
  for a prettier presentation, but it's not necessary)
6 oz. (1½ cups) cheddar cheese, shredded
  and divided
2 T. catsup
Salt and pepper to taste

Preheat the oven to 350°.

Trim the ends of the zucchini; cut them in half lengthwise and then scoop out the pulp, leaving a ½-inch shell. Set aside the zucchini "boats" for now. Finely chop the pulp.

In a skillet, cook the zucchini pulp, ground beef, onion, mushrooms, and bell pepper over medium heat, stirring occasionally and breaking up the meat, until the meat is no longer pink; drain.

Remove the meat mixture from the heat and add half of the cheese, catsup, salt, and pepper; mix well.

Spoon the meat mixture into the zucchini shells; sprinkle on the remaining cheddar cheese and place the zucchini boats into a large greased baking dish.

Bake for 25 to 30 minutes or until the meat mixture is bubbling and the zucchini is tender.

Serves 6

A meal rarely feels complete without that extra something to go along with the main dish, and that's where veggies and side dishes shine. Side dishes go a long way toward assuaging hunger pangs and rounding out a meal.

If you keep a garden, selecting fresh vegetables is as easy as walking outside and deciding what's for dinner. It takes a bit more effort to go to the store or shop the local farmer's market, but the results are worth it. Learn what's in season to take advantage of lower prices and easy availability.

Some of my family's favorites include Corn and Green Chile Rice, Sautéed Swiss Chard, Stewed Tomatoes and Dumplings, and Tomatoes with Pine Nuts and Parsley.

Enjoy!

VEGETABLES AND SIDE DISHES

Baked Beans

2 cups dried navy (small white) beans	1½ T. salt
½ lb. bacon, diced	1 cup brown sugar
½ cup catsup	½ cup granulated sugar
1 medium onion, chopped	1 pint tomato juice

Place the beans in a large stockpot and add enough water to cover. Boil the beans for 5 minutes, then cover the pot, turn off the heat, and let them sit for 1 hour. Drain the beans and cover them again with fresh water. Place them back on the stove and simmer them until they are cooked, about 2 hours, adding boiling water as needed to keep them covered. When the beans are tender, drain most of the water, then add the remaining ingredients; stir to mix thoroughly.

Pour the bean mixture into a large bean pot or ovenproof casserole dish and bake at 325°, uncovered, for about 2 hours, adding a bit of boiling water if needed so they don't dry out and scorch on the bottom.

Baked beans are . . . well . . . *baked.* But I confess that we sometimes eat this without baking because we like our beans runny. So suit yourself: Bake them for the allotted time, bake them for half the time, or don't bake them at all. They'll be good no matter what you decide.

Makes 12 (½-cup) servings

Baked Beets in Béchamel Sauce

4 medium beets, peeled and out into ¼-inch slices	3 T. flour
½ cup water	1 cup milk
3 T. butter	¼ cup dry white wine
1 shallot, minced	Salt and pepper to taste
	Pinch of nutmeg

Preheat the oven to 425°.

Arrange the beets in a large baking dish. Add the water, cover tightly with aluminum foil, and bake for about 45 minutes or until the beets are fork tender.

Meanwhile, melt the butter in a saucepan over medium heat. Add the shallot and sauté until softened, about 3 minutes. Stir in the flour. Slowly whisk in the milk and wine, and then bring the mixture to a gentle boil as it thickens.

Remove the sauce from the heat and add salt and pepper to taste and a pinch of nutmeg. Pour the sauce over the beets in the baking dish and continue to bake, uncovered this time, for about 10 minutes or until the sauce is bubbling and golden brown around the edges.

Serves 4 to 6

Vegetables
suited for long-term winter storage include winter squash (think pumpkin, spaghetti squash, delicata, acorn, butternut, and Hubbard), potatoes and sweet potatoes, beets, cabbage, carrots, onions, garlic, turnips, rutabagas, radishes, apples, and citrus fruit, including lemons and limes.

Baked Macaroni and Cheese

½ cup (1 stick) butter, softened to room
  temperature and divided
½ cup Panko bread crumbs
4 cups uncooked elbow macaroni noodles
¼ cup flour

3 cups whole milk
1½ tsp. dry mustard
4 cups shredded cheddar cheese
1½ tsp. salt
¼ tsp. pepper

Melt 2 tablespoons of the butter in a small bowl, then pour in the bread crumbs and stir together with a fork; set aside for now.

Cook the macaroni according to the package directions, then drain the water.

Preheat the oven to 350°.

Using 2 tablespoons of the butter, grease the bottom and sides of a large baking pan.

In a large pot, melt the remaining ¼ cup of butter over medium-low heat and then sprinkle in the flour, whisking as you do so. Turn the heat to about medium and cook the roux, whisking all the while, for 1 minute. Pour in the milk, continuing to whisk, then add the mustard and keep whisking until the sauce boils and thickens slightly. Reduce the heat to your lowest setting, add the cheese, and stir to melt. Add the salt and pepper and stir to combine. Pour in the drained, cooked macaroni and mix carefully but thoroughly.

Pour the macaroni and cheese into the buttered baking pan and top with the buttered bread crumbs.

Bake for 15 minutes.

Serves 10 to 12

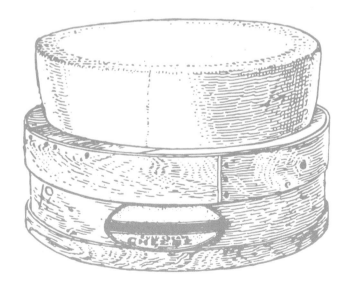

Corn and Green Chile Rice

3 cups cooked long-grain white rice
1 cup cottage cheese
2 cups fresh or frozen corn, thawed
1 cup sour cream

1 or 2 (4½ oz.) cans chopped green chiles, drained, to taste
1 cup (4 oz.) shredded cheddar or Mexican blend cheese

Preheat the oven to 375°.

Grease a 2-quart casserole with nonstick cooking spray or butter.

In a large mixing bowl, combine all the ingredients except the cheese; mix well. Spoon the rice mixture into the prepared casserole dish and sprinkle the cheese over the top.

Bake, uncovered, for 30 to 35 minutes or until the casserole is thoroughly heated and the cheese is melted. (If the cheese on top of the casserole begins to look too brown, you can cover the baking dish with aluminum foil and finish baking.)

Serves 8 to 10

Tip: *This is a great use for leftover cooked rice, but if you don't have any, simply cook 1 cup of long-grain dry rice in 2 cups of water, according to package directions, and then continue as directed in this recipe.*

Creamy Potato Casserole

1 (32 oz.) package hash browns, thawed
1½ cups sour cream
¾ cup (1½ sticks) melted butter, divided
1½ cups shredded cheddar cheese

½ cup onion, finely diced
1 (10½ oz.) can cream of mushroom soup
Salt and pepper to taste
2 cups crushed cornflakes

In a large mixing bowl, stir together the hash browns, sour cream, ½ cup melted butter, cheese, onion, soup, salt, and pepper. Pour the mixture into a 9 x 13-inch baking dish that has been lightly greased with cooking spray or butter. Mix together the remaining ¼ cup of the melted butter and the cornflakes and sprinkle over the top of the dish.

Bake at 350° for 1 hour.

Serves 8 to 10

Dutch Slaw

1 head cabbage
½ cup heavy cream
1 tsp. salt

½ cup sugar
½ cup vinegar

Discard the outer leaves of cabbage. Wash the remainder of the cabbage, drain well, and then shred the leaves and place all the cabbage in a large bowl.

In a small bowl, mix together the cream, salt, sugar, and vinegar and beat very well.

Just before serving, pour the dressing over the cabbage and mix well.

Serves 8 to 10

Tip: *This is a classic coleslaw. If desired, you can add a bit of diced onion, carrot, or bell pepper. For a change of pace, I sometimes add a can of drained mandarin oranges. Delicious!*

Line your crisper drawer with paper towels to keep whole fruits and vegetables fresh longer.

Eggplant, Zucchini, and Tomato Casserole

1 lb. eggplant
1 lb. zucchini
¼ cup butter
1 onion, minced
¾ lb. whole tomatoes

Salt and pepper to taste
1 cup shredded cheddar cheese
¼ cup panko bread crumbs (or any unflavored
    coarse dry bread crumbs)

Preheat the oven to 350°.

Peel the eggplant and then cut it into ½-inch cubes.

Slice the zucchini diagonally into ½-inch-thick pieces, removing the stem.

Place the eggplant and zucchini into a large pot along with 2 cups of water and 1 tsp. of salt; bring to a boil and then cover and cook for about 5 minutes more. Drain the vegetables very well; set aside for now while continuing to drain.

In the same large pot, melt the butter over medium-low heat. Add the minced onion and sauté until the onions are tender, about 15 minutes, then remove from the heat.

Skin the tomatoes and cut them into bite-size chunks. Add the tomatoes and the eggplant mixture to the pot and gently stir, doing your best to keep the pieces intact. Add salt and pepper to taste.

Place the entire mixture into a fairly shallow baking dish (I use an oval, 2½-quart casserole dish) that has been buttered or greased. Sprinkle the cheese and panko bread crumbs over the top of the vegetable mixture; cover with aluminum foil, and then bake for 30 minutes. Remove the foil and bake uncovered for 5 to 10 minutes more (until the liquid is evaporated). Remove the dish from the oven and let it stand for 5 minutes before serving.

Serves 6 to 8

German Potato Salad

SALAD
8 potatoes, peeled, cubed
    and boiled
1 stalk celery, chopped
2 hard-boiled eggs
1 onion, chopped
1 T. fresh parsley, minced

DRESSING
4 slices bacon, diced
2 eggs, well beaten
1 cup sugar
½ cup vinegar
½ cup cold water
½ tsp. salt

¼ tsp. dry mustard
½ tsp. salt
¼ tsp. pepper

Combine all the salad ingredients in a large bowl and then prepare the dressing.

Fry the bacon in a skillet until crisp. Reserve the grease in the pan, but remove the bacon to a paper-towel-lined plate to drain. Crumble it into bacon bits and add them to the salad. In a small bowl, beat together the eggs, sugar, vinegar, water, and spices. Pour the mixture into the hot bacon grease and cook, stirring, until the mixture thickens, about 10 minutes. Pour the dressing over the potato mixture and mix gently. Refrigerate the salad for several hours before serving, or eat it as soon as it has cooled down to room temperature.

Serves 10

Honey Glazed Carrots

1 lb. carrots
2 T. butter
3 T. brown sugar
2 T. honey

1 T. lemon juice
Salt and pepper to taste
½ to 1 tsp. dried thyme leaves (optional)

Peel, rinse, and cut the carrots into ½-inch slices and then place them in a medium saucepan. Cover the carrots with water and add a pinch of salt. Bring them to a boil; reduce the heat, cover the pot, and continue cooking for about 15 minutes or until the carrots are tender. Drain the water and set the carrots aside.

In the same saucepan, melt the butter over medium-low heat. Add the brown sugar and honey and cook, stirring, until the sugar is dissolved and the syrup is hot. Stir in the lemon juice and then gently stir in the carrots, being careful to coat them well. Continue cooking the carrots, stirring gently, until the carrots are glazed, about 10 minutes.

Remove the pan from the heat, add salt and pepper to taste, and sprinkle the thyme over the carrots. Serve immediately.

Serves 4 to 6

Layered Lettuce and Pea Salad

1 head iceberg lettuce, coarsely shredded
    or chopped
½ cup celery, sliced
¼ cup onion, diced
½ cup bell peppers (any color), chopped

1 (10 oz.) package frozen peas, or about
    2 cups fresh peas
2 cups mayonnaise
½ cup shredded cheddar cheese
6 slices bacon, cooked and chopped, or
    about ½ cup bacon bits, more or less

In a casserole dish or large salad bowl, layer the first 6 ingredients in the order given, then cover and refrigerate for at least 6 hours. When you are ready to serve the salad, sprinkle on the cheese and bacon bits.

Serves 8 to 10

Wrap your lettuce in aluminum foil (tightly but gently) to keep fresh for weeks. I use this technique for celery also and it works amazingly well. If you don't use aluminum foil, you can roll your cleaned and dried leafy greens (salad spinners work well) into a towel and refrigerate.

Potato Stuffing

6 cups mashed potatoes, room temperature
3 eggs, beaten
1 stick (½ cup) butter
½ cup onion, minced
1 cup celery, diced

1 quart bread cubes
½ cup fresh parsley, minced
Salt and pepper to taste
Paprika (optional)

In a large mixing bowl, stir together the mashed potatoes and beaten eggs.

In a large saucepan, melt the butter over medium heat, then sauté the onion and celery. Add the bread cubes and toast for several minutes, carefully and constantly stirring. Remove from the heat and add the parsley, salt, pepper.

Combine the bread mixture with the mashed potato mixture and mix thoroughly. Spread it all in a large greased roasting pan, and sprinkle with paprika and pats of butter if desired. Bake at 350° for 1 hour or until the stuffing is baked through and the top is golden.

Makes about 3 quarts

Rice Pilaf

2½ cups water
3 to 4 chicken, beef, or vegetable bouillon cubes
4 T. butter, more or less

1½ cups uncooked vermicelli or spaghetti noodles, broken into small pieces (see note below)
1 cup uncooked white rice (see note below)

In a medium pot, add the water and bouillon cubes and bring to a simmer; the bouillon cubes will dissolve as the water boils.

Meanwhile, in a large pot, melt the butter over medium heat. Add the vermicelli and brown, stirring constantly to keep the pieces from burning. Turn down the heat and then add the rice and boiling broth; stir to mix.

Cover the pot and simmer for about 20 to 25 minutes or until the rice is cooked through and soft. Add salt and pepper as needed, and a bit more butter if desired, and serve.

Serves about 6

Note: *You can make a larger or smaller recipe as needed. Just remember to use the same amount of water as the combined amount of uncooked vermicelli and rice, and use one or so bouillon cubes per cup of water.*

Roasted Brussels Sprouts with Hazelnuts and Parmesan

3 T. butter
½ tsp. salt
½ tsp. pepper

1½ lbs. brussels sprouts, trimmed and
   quartered lengthwise
¼ cup chopped hazelnuts
2 T. shredded Parmesan cheese

Preheat the oven to 450°.

In a small saucepan, melt the butter until it is bubbling but not too brown. Remove the pan from the heat and stir in the salt and pepper.

Place the brussels sprouts and hazelnuts on a lightly greased baking sheet; drizzle the melted butter over the sprouts and hazelnuts and gently toss to coat. Roast the sprouts for 12 to 15 minutes or until they are tender, stirring occasionally. You can bake them a bit longer if you prefer a slight char on the sprouts.

Remove them from the oven and immediately sprinkle with Parmesan cheese.

Serves 6

Harvest produce
early in the morning, and it will be
crisper, juicier, and sweeter.

Roasted Green Beans

2 lbs. fresh green beans	4 cloves garlic, minced
Olive oil	Salt and pepper to taste

Preheat the oven to 400°.

Snip the ends of the green beans and lay them in a single layer on a rimmed baking sheet. Spray or drizzle the beans with olive oil, then sprinkle the garlic as evenly as possible over the beans.

Place the tray in the oven and roast for about 20 minutes (depending on how dark of a roast you prefer), turning the beans at least once during the baking process. When the green beans begin to wrinkle and develop a bit of char, they are ready.

Serves 6 to 8

Tip: *You can substitute fresh asparagus for the green beans, but they will need a shorter roasting time, about 10 to 15 minutes, depending on the thickness of the spears.*

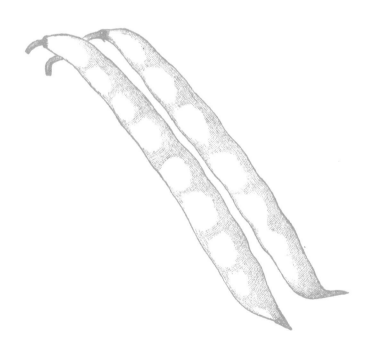

Sautéed Swiss Chard

6 stalks Swiss chard (rainbow chard, often called Neon Lights, is beautiful in this recipe)
1 T. olive oil
1 tsp. butter
¼ cup onion, chopped

¼ cup dry white wine (you can substitute water, chicken broth, or vegetable broth)
Salt and pepper to taste
1 tomato, diced (optional)
4 T. shredded Parmesan cheese, to taste

Clean and separate the Swiss chard stalks from the leaves. Chop the stalks and leaves, keeping them separate.

Add the oil and butter to a sauté pan and heat on medium. Add the onion and stalks of chard and cook, stirring, for about 4 minutes. Add the wine, chopped leaves, salt, and pepper and continue cooking, stirring occasionally, for another 3 minutes. Remove from the heat.

Add the diced tomato to the chard and quickly but gently stir to mix. Sprinkle the Parmesan cheese over the top. Cover the pan and allow the chard to rest for a minute or two before serving so the tomatoes become warm and the Parmesan cheese melts a bit.

Serves 4 to 6

Scalloped Corn Casserole

1 quart corn (canned and drained, frozen corn that has been thawed, or fresh cooked)
1 cup cracker crumbs or bread crumbs

2 eggs
½ cup milk
Salt and pepper to taste

Preheat the oven to 350°.

Place the corn and crumbs in layers in a buttered casserole dish, keeping out a bit of crumbs to sprinkle on top.

In a small mixing bowl, beat the eggs well; add the milk, salt, and pepper. Carefully pour the egg mixture over the corn and crumbs, then top with the remaining crumbs and bake for 20 minutes or until bubbly and golden on top.

Makes 8 (½ cup) servings

Scalloped Potatoes

6 large russet potatoes, peeled and thinly sliced
9 T. flour, divided
6 T. cold butter, divided and finely cubed

1 quart milk (more or less)
Salt and pepper to taste
¾ cup cheddar cheese (optional)

Preheat the oven to 425°.

Butter a 9 x 13-inch baking dish. Add a third of the potatoes to the dish and sprinkle with a third (3 T.) of the flour and a third (2 T.) of the butter. Repeat these layers two more times, then carefully pour in the milk until it covers about ¾ of the potatoes.

Bake in the preheated oven for 15 minutes. Reduce the heat to 375° and continue baking until done, about another 45 to 60 minutes. If desired, during the last 15 minutes, sprinkle the cheddar cheese on top and finish baking.

Serves 6 to 8

Stewed Tomatoes and Dumplings

TOMATOES
¼ cup butter
½ cup onion, chopped
¼ cup celery, chopped
2 quarts home-canned tomatoes, undrained,
　　or 1 (28 oz.) can whole tomatoes, coarsely
　　chopped with juice
2 tsp. brown sugar
½ tsp. salt
½ tsp. dried basil
½ tsp. pepper

DUMPLINGS
1 cup flour
1½ tsp. baking powder
½ tsp. salt
1 T. butter
1 egg, beaten
6 T. milk
1 T. fresh minced parsley, or 1 heaping tsp.
　　dried parsley

For the stewed tomatoes:

In a medium-large saucepan, melt the butter and sauté the onion and celery for about 3 minutes. Add the tomatoes with their juice, brown sugar, and seasonings, and bring to a boil. Simmer uncovered for several minutes.

For the dumplings:

In a medium mixing bowl, combine the flour, baking powder, and salt. Cut in the butter using a pastry blender or two knives until the mixture resembles coarse crumbs. Add the egg, milk, and parsley to the bowl and blend lightly without overmixing. To form the dumplings, drop tablespoonfuls of dough into the simmering tomato mixture. Cover the pot tightly and cook over medium-low heat for 20 minutes. (Don't lift the lid during cooking.) Serve in bowls, topped with a pat of butter if desired.

Serves 6

Sweet Potato Fries

....

4 sweet potatoes, skinned and sliced into long,
  thin strips
2 to 3 T. oil

1 tsp. salt
Large pinch hot ground pepper,
  such as cayenne

Preheat the oven to 450°.

Place the potato slices in a gallon-sized freezer bag and drizzle with the oil, salt, and pepper. Close the bag and shake it to coat the slices as evenly as possible.

Spread the potato slices evenly on a rimmed baking sheet and bake for about 20 minutes or until tender and lightly browned, turning once.

Serves 4 to 6

Tip: *You can use this recipe with russet potatoes as well, but I usually leave out the hot pepper and instead add some non-salt seasoning or paprika. Also, we like our fries a bit on the crispy side, so I tend to roast them a bit longer, depending on the thickness of the slices.*

Tomatoes with Pine Nuts and Parsley

6 ripe tomatoes
2 T. olive oil
½ cup pine nuts
4 T. butter

2 cloves garlic, minced
1 cup fresh parsley, minced
Pinch of salt

Halve and seed the tomatoes, sprinkle the cut sides with salt, and place them on a folded towel (or paper towels) on the counter to drain, cut side down, for about 30 minutes.

Preheat the oven to 350°.

In a medium skillet, sauté the tomatoes in the olive oil for 2 to 3 minutes on each side or until they are just beginning to soften. Transfer the tomatoes, cut side up, to a baking dish (the size will vary depending on how big your tomatoes are) and place them in the oven to keep warm.

In the same skillet, turn the heat to medium. Add the pine nuts and sauté for about 2 minutes or until they are lightly colored. Use a slotted spoon to transfer them to paper towels to drain.

Now, melt the butter in the skillet (you may need to turn the heat down a bit so the butter doesn't brown). Next, add the garlic and parsley plus a pinch of salt. Sauté, stirring or shaking the pan, for several minutes.

Remove the tomatoes from the oven, spoon the parsley mixture over the tomatoes, and top them with the pine nuts. They are ready to serve immediately, or you can return them to the oven for about 5 minutes if they need a bit more cooking time.

Serves 6, with two halves each

Learn to safely forage in your area. Harvesting from the wild can be especially helpful in early spring before main gardens get growing and again in the fall, at the peak of harvest. Some examples of easy foraging in my area include dandelions, lamb's quarter, watercress, blackberries, huckleberries, mushrooms, elderberries (cook them or juice them), and wild rosehips. As with any foraging, learn from an expert before going out on your own.

Rolls and buns may take a bit more time than some offerings, but the results are worth the effort. They are good any day of the week but particularly shine when part of a special meal. Homemade rolls and buns just seem to say, "Celebrate!"

Even if you are a seasoned bread baker, you may not have tried expanding your repertoire to include the recipes in this section. But do give them a try, and once you do, the next step is to play around with the ingredients. Use different types of flour. Add some of this or a pinch of that—just use what's available or what seems like a good addition to the recipe. You may be pleasantly surprised with the results.

Try the Mashed Potato Rolls, Hamburger Buns, or the Overnight Refrigerator Butter Crescent Rolls (they don't need kneading!) to get started. If I don't miss my guess, you'll wonder why you would ever eat store-bought rolls or buns again. They are that good!

Black Raspberry Sweet Rolls

ROLLS

3½ to 4 cups all-purpose
    flour, divided
½ cup sugar
1 tsp. salt
4½ tsp. (2 packages) active
    dry yeast
1 cup milk
½ cup (1 stick) butter
2 eggs

TOPPING

¼ cup (½ stick) butter, melted
½ cup black raspberry preserves
    (you can also use red raspberry,
    blackberry, or other preserves)

GLAZE

1 cup powdered sugar
2 to 3 T. milk

For the rolls:

In a large bowl, whisk together 1½ cups flour with the sugar, salt, and yeast.

In a small saucepan, heat the milk and butter until they reach about 115° on a kitchen thermometer. Pour the milk mixture into the flour mixture and blend on low speed until incorporated. Add the eggs and blend again, and then beat the dough on medium speed for 3 minutes. Gradually stir in additional flour (about 2 cups should do it) until the dough pulls away from the sides of the bowl.

Turn out the dough on a floured work surface and knead it for about 4 to 5 minutes, adding small amounts of flour as needed to keep the dough from sticking. Place the dough in a large greased bowl, turning the dough so the entire surface is greased. Cover the bowl and let the dough rise about an hour, until it has doubled in volume.

Punch down the dough and then turn it out onto a lightly floured work surface. Divide the dough into 24 pieces. Roll each piece into a 15-inch rope.

Grease cookie sheets (you will probably need 3 total) and, working directly on the prepared cookie sheet, loosely coil each rope into a circle, tucking the ends underneath. Cover and let the rolls rise until doubled, about 20 to 30 minutes. Meanwhile, preheat the oven to 350°.

For the topping:

After the rolls have risen, gently brush them with the melted butter (save the leftover butter to brush the rolls again after baking). Make a deep indent with your thumb or knuckle in the center of each roll. Spoon about 1 teaspoon of the preserves into each thumbprint.

Bake for about 15 to 20 minutes or until done and the tops are a light golden brown. Remove the rolls from the cookie sheets immediately after baking and brush them a second time with the leftover melted butter. Allow the rolls to cool.

For the glaze:

In a small bowl, mix together the powdered sugar and milk and then drizzle the glaze over the cooled rolls.

Makes 24 rolls

Butter Pan Rolls

....

4½ tsp. (2 packages) active dry yeast
½ cup warm water (about 110°)
4½ cups all-purpose flour, divided
¼ cup sugar
1 tsp. salt

1 cup (2 sticks) plus 2 T. (¼ stick) butter,
  melted and cooled, divided
1 egg, beaten
1 cup warm milk (about 110°)

In a medium bowl, dissolve the yeast in the warm water; allow it to stand until bubbly, about 10 to 15 minutes.

In a large bowl, whisk together 2 cups of the flour with the sugar and salt. Add 6 tablespoons of the melted butter, the egg, the yeast mixture, and the warm milk. Beat for 5 minutes on medium speed.

Gradually beat in the remaining flour. Cover the bowl and let the dough rise until doubled, about 45 minutes to an hour.

Pour half of the remaining butter (about 6 tablespoons) into a 9 x 13-inch baking pan, making sure to coat the entire bottom of the pan. (You may need to reliquefy the butter and then cool it again to barely warm.) Punch down the dough and then drop by spoonfuls into the buttered pan. There should be enough batter to make 15 rolls. Drizzle the remaining butter over the dough. Cover the pan loosely with plastic wrap and let the dough rise again until it is almost doubled, about 30 minutes. Meanwhile, preheat the oven to 425°.

Bake the rolls for 12 to 17 minutes or until done.

Makes 15 rolls

Butterscotch Rolls

½ cup (1 stick) butter, melted
1½ cups brown sugar
2½ cups all-purpose or pastry flour
3½ tsp. baking powder
1 tsp. salt

¼ cup sugar
5 T. shortening
½ cup milk
1 egg, well beaten

Preheat the oven to 400°.

Lightly grease 24 muffin cups. Put 1 teaspoon of melted butter and 1 teaspoon of brown sugar into the bottom of each muffin cup. You won't use all the melted butter and brown sugar; the rest will be spread on the dough (see below).

In a large bowl, whisk together the flour, baking powder, salt, and sugar. Cut in the shortening until it resembles coarse crumbs.

In a small bowl, mix together the milk and egg, then add the liquid to the flour mixture and stir until combined. Turn out the dough onto a floured surface and knead 20 times. Roll the dough into a rectangle that is about 12 inches long and ¼ inch thick. Spread the remaining melted butter on the dough and then sprinkle with the remaining brown sugar. Roll up the dough jelly-roll style (from the long side), cut it into ½-inch-thick pieces, and place the pieces in the pre-pared muffin pans.

Bake for 20 to 25 minutes or until done.

Makes 24 rolls

Cheese Rolls

2 cups all-purpose flour, plus more for rolling
5 tsp. baking powder
1 tsp. salt
2 T. shortening

¾ cup milk
1 cup grated cheese, such as cheddar, Swiss,
   or Monterey Jack

Preheat the oven to 450°.

In a large bowl, whisk together the flour, baking powder, and salt. Cut in the shortening until the mixture resembles coarse crumbs. Gradually add the milk, and mix to form a soft dough. Turn out the dough onto a floured work surface and roll the dough into a thin rectangle, then sprinkle on the cheese.

Beginning with one of the long sides, roll the dough into a log, like a jelly roll. Cut the log into 1-inch-thick pieces and place them, cut side up, on a greased baking sheet.

Bake for 12 minutes or until done.

Makes about 12 rolls

Cinnamon Fans

DOUGH

3 cups all-purpose flour,
  plus more for kneading
1 tsp. salt
4 tsp. baking powder

1 tsp. cream of tartar
⅓ cup sugar
¾ cup shortening
1 cup milk

FILLING

½ cup (1 stick) butter, melted
  and cooled
½ cup sugar
2 T. cinnamon

Preheat the oven to 400°.

Grease a 12-cup muffin pan and set it aside.

For the dough:

Whisk together the flour, salt, baking powder, cream of tartar, and sugar. Cut in the shortening until the mixture resembles coarse crumbs. Add the milk and stir until just combined. Turn out the dough onto a lightly floured surface and knead it gently for a half-minute.

Roll out the dough into a rectangle that is about 8 x 24 inches and about ¼ inch thick.

For the filling:

Spread the melted butter evenly on the dough. Mix together the sugar and cinnamon and then sprinkle the mixture evenly over the buttered dough.

Cut the dough into 4 long strips, each about 2 inches wide and 24 inches long. Stack the 4 strips on top of one another and then cut the stack into 12 equal pieces, each about 2 inches wide. Place the pieces into the greased muffin cups on their sides so that each treat fans out.

Bake for 12 minutes or until golden brown.

Makes 12 fans

Cinnamon Rolls

DOUGH
⅓ cup butter
1 (12 oz.) can evaporated milk
¾ cup sugar
3 T. active dry yeast
3 eggs
1 T. salt
4 cups all-purpose flour, plus more for kneading

FILLING
¾ cup (1½ sticks) butter, softened
2 to 3 cups sugar
Cinnamon, to taste
Raisins and chopped nuts (optional)

For the dough:

In a small saucepan, heat the butter and evaporated milk until it reaches 115°.

In a large mixing bowl, mix together the evaporated milk mixture, sugar, and yeast. Let the mixture rest for 5 minutes so the yeast can begin to work. Add the eggs one at a time, mixing well after each addition. Add the salt and mix well. Slowly add the flour, one cup at a time, mixing well after each addition. Continue adding the flour until the dough begins to pull away from the sides of the bowl and forms a ball. (You may not need quite all the flour.)

Turn out the dough onto a lightly floured work surface and knead for 10 minutes, using as little flour as possible to keep the dough from sticking. Place the dough into a large greased bowl, turning the dough so the entire surface is greased. Cover the dough and let it rise until doubled, about 1 to 1½ hours.

For the filling:

On a floured surface, roll out the dough into a rectangle that is about 18 inches long and ½-inch thick. Spread the surface with the butter, then sprinkle on the sugar. Sprinkle the cinnamon atop the sugar and then scatter the raisins and nuts on top (if using). Starting at one of the long sides, roll dough into a log, then cut it into about 24 rolls. Place the rolls cut side up on 2 greased jelly roll pans. Cover the pans with plastic wrap, and let the rolls rise again until doubled, about 45 minutes. Meanwhile, preheat the oven to 350°.

Bake the rolls for about 25 minutes or until done.

Makes 24 rolls

Note: *These are great plain, but you can also top them with a glaze made by mixing ½ cup of powdered sugar with 2 to 3 teaspoons of milk.*

Buy yeast in bulk.
You can get inexpensive 2-pound packages from some big-box stores, and they last for many months in the refrigerator.

Cracked Wheat Potato Rolls

¾ cup cracked wheat
1 cup (2 sticks) butter
3 cups boiling water
7 cups all-purpose flour, more or less, divided
2 T. yeast
⅔ cup instant potato flakes

½ cup nonfat dry milk
⅔ cup sugar
1 T. salt
2 T. wheat germ (optional)
2 eggs

In a large bowl, combine the cracked wheat, butter, and boiling water. Let the bowl sit on the counter until it has cooled to lukewarm. Add 2 cups of the flour and all remaining ingredients to the bowl with the cracked wheat. Beat the batter with an electric mixer on medium speed for 3 minutes. Gradually add the remaining flour a cup at a time and stir by hand until the dough pulls away from the sides of the bowl. You may not need quite all of the flour.

Turn out the dough onto a floured work surface and knead for about 8 minutes. Grease a different large bowl and place the dough inside, turning it so the entire surface of the dough is greased. Cover the bowl and let the dough rise until doubled, about 1½ hours.

Punch down the dough and let it rest for about 5 minutes. Shape into round rolls and place on two greased baking sheets. Cover and let rise for 30 minutes. Meanwhile, preheat the oven to 350°.

Bake the rolls for 15 to 20 minutes or until done.

Makes 45 to 48 rolls, any extras will freeze well

Dill Rolls

3 to 3½ cups all-purpose flour, divided
¼ cup sugar
1 tsp. dill weed
1 tsp. salt

2¼ tsp. (1 package) active dry yeast
1½ cups milk
⅓ cup butter
1 egg

In a large bowl, whisk together 1½ cups of the flour with the sugar, dill weed, salt, and yeast.

In a small saucepan, heat the milk and butter until warm (120° to 130°). Add the warm milk mixture and the egg to the flour mixture and blend on low speed until moistened, then beat on medium speed for 3 minutes. Stir in the additional flour to make a stiff batter. Cover the bowl with a towel and let the batter rise until doubled, about 45 to 60 minutes.

Grease 18 muffin cups. Stir down the batter and then spoon it into the prepared muffin cups. Each cup should be about ⅔ full. Cover the pans with a towel and let the rolls rise until doubled, about 35 to 45 minutes. Meanwhile, preheat the oven to 400°.

Bake the rolls for 15 to 20 minutes or until done. Remove them from the pans to cool on a wire rack.

Makes 18 rolls

German Sweet Rolls

4½ cups all-purpose flour, divided
1 cup sugar
2 tsp. cream of tartar
1 tsp. salt
1 tsp. baking soda
½ cup shortening

½ cup (1 stick) butter
2 eggs, divided
¼ cup milk
¼ cup water
1 cup brown sugar

Preheat the oven to 375°.

In a large mixing bowl, whisk 4 cups of the flour with the sugar, cream of tartar, salt, and baking soda. Cut in the shortening and butter until the mixture resembles coarse crumbs. Beat one of the eggs and add it to the flour mixture, along with the milk and water, to form a soft dough.

In another bowl, beat the other egg, then mix in the brown sugar and the final ½ cup of flour. Set this aside.

Roll the dough into a ½-inch-thick rectangle that is about 24 inches long. Spread the brown sugar mixture on top of the dough. Beginning with one of the long ends, roll up the dough like a jelly roll and cut slices that are about 1 inch thick. Place the rolls cut side up, about 2 inches apart, on greased baking sheets.

Bake for 8 to 10 minutes or until done.

Makes 24 rolls

Hamburger or Hot Dog Buns

2 T. active dry yeast
1 cup plus 2 T. warm water (about 110°)
⅓ cup cooking oil
¼ cup sugar

1 egg
1 tsp. salt
3 to 3½ cups all-purpose flour

In a large bowl, dissolve the yeast in the warm water. Add the cooking oil and sugar and mix again. Let the mixture sit until the yeast begins to bubble, about 10 minutes.

Add the egg, salt, and 3 cups of flour to form a soft dough. Add the extra flour if the dough is too sticky. Turn out the dough onto a floured surface and knead it for about 5 minutes. Do not let the dough rise.

Divide the dough into 12 pieces and shape each piece as desired: into a ball for a hamburger bun or a log for a hot dog bun. Place the buns 3 inches apart on greased cookie sheets. Cover the buns and let the dough rest for 15 minutes. Meanwhile, preheat the oven to 425°.

Bake for 8 to 12 minutes or until they are done and the tops are golden brown. Cool the buns on wire racks and then slice them in half lengthwise to serve.

Makes 12 buns

Hoagie Rolls

3 cups warm water, divided
2¼ tsp. (1 package) active dry yeast
2 T. sugar, divided

¼ cup cooking oil
1 T. salt
8 to 8½ cups all-purpose flour, divided

Fill a large bowl with ½ cup warm water (about 110°). Dissolve the yeast and 1 tablespoon of the sugar in the water; let stand until bubbly, about 5 to 10 minutes. Add the remaining water and sugar to the bowl, and then stir in the oil, salt, and 4 cups of the flour. Using an electric mixer, beat the batter on medium speed for 3 minutes. (You can also do this step by hand using a large wooden spoon.) Stir in enough of the remaining flour to form a soft dough.

Turn out the dough onto a floured work surface and knead it for about 8 minutes, adding very small amounts of flour as needed to prevent sticking. Place the ball of kneaded dough into a greased bowl, turning the dough so the entire surface is greased. Cover the bowl and let the dough rise until doubled, about 1 hour.

Punch down the dough and turn it out onto a lightly floured surface. Divide the dough into 18 equal pieces. Shape each piece of dough into an oval and place the rolls 2 inches apart on greased baking sheets. With a very sharp knife or kitchen scissors, slash the top of each piece ¼ inch deep. Cover the rolls with a towel and let them rise again for 20 minutes. Meanwhile, preheat the oven to 400°.

Bake the rolls for 13 to 18 minutes or until they are a light golden color and done. Cool the rolls on wire racks and then slice them in half lengthwise to serve.

Makes 18 rolls

Make-Ahead Dinner Rolls

2¼ tsp. (1 package) active dry yeast
2 T. warm water (about 110°)
1 cup very hot water (it doesn't have to be boiling)
1 tsp. salt

¾ cup shortening
¼ cup sugar
1 egg, well beaten
3½ cups all-purpose flour

In a small bowl, combine the yeast with the warm water and set it aside until it is bubbly, about 10 minutes.

In a large mixing bowl, combine the hot water, salt, shortening, and sugar and mix well to dissolve the salt and sugar and melt the shortening. Cool the mixture to lukewarm.

When the hot water mixture is lukewarm, add the yeast mixture to the now lukewarm mixture, stir, and then add the beaten egg followed by half of the flour. Beat the batter at high speed for 3 minutes.

With a wooden spoon, stir in more of the flour, enough to make the dough easy to handle. (It will be softer than regular kneaded dough.) Cover and store this dough in the refrigerator for up to a week.

When you want to bake some dinner rolls, take out the amount of dough needed. Shape the dough into balls that are slightly larger than a golf ball, and put them in a greased baking pan or in greased muffin cups. Cover them and let them rise in a warm place until the dough warms up and doubles in bulk, about 2 to 2½ hours.

Preheat the oven to 425° and bake the rolls for 12 to 15 minutes or until done.

Makes 18 rolls

Maple Buns

....

DOUGH	FILLING	GLAZE
4½ tsp. (2 packages) active dry yeast	2 T. (¼ stick) butter, softened	½ cup powdered sugar
1¼ cups warm milk (about 110°)	¼ cup brown sugar	⅛ tsp. maple flavoring
3½ to 4 cups all-purpose flour, divided	½ tsp. maple flavoring	2 to 3 tsp. milk
½ cup rolled oats		
¼ cup sugar		
¼ cup brown sugar		
½ tsp. salt		
¼ cup cooking oil		

For the dough:

In a small bowl, dissolve the yeast in the warm milk, and let it sit until the mixture is a bit bubbly.

In a large bowl, whisk 1 cup of the flour with the rolled oats, sugar, brown sugar, and salt until well blended. Pour the yeast mixture and the cooking oil into the flour mixture. Stir it until it is well blended, then beat the batter on medium speed for 3 minutes. Gradually stir in most of the remaining flour, just enough so that the dough pulls away from the sides of the bowl.

Turn out the dough onto a floured surface and knead it for about 10 minutes, adding flour as needed to prevent sticking. Cover the dough with plastic wrap or a large upturned bowl and let it rest for 25 minutes.

For the filling:

Roll the dough into a 12 x 16-inch rectangle. Spread the dough with the softened butter. Mix together the brown sugar and the maple flavoring, and then sprinkle the mixture over the buttered dough. Starting with a 12-inch side, roll the dough into a tight log. Cut the log into 12 1-inch pieces. Place them in a greased 13 x 9-inch baking pan or jelly roll pan. Cover the pan and let the dough rise until doubled, about an hour. Meanwhile, preheat the oven to 350°.

Bake the rolls for 20 to 30 minutes or until done. Cool them in the pan for 1 to 2 minutes and then remove the buns from the pan. Immediately make the glaze.

For the glaze:

Whisk together all the glaze ingredients and then drizzle the glaze over the warm buns.

Makes 12 buns

Mashed Potato Rolls

2¼ tsp. (1 package) active dry yeast
¼ cup warm water (about 110°)
1¾ cups warm milk (about 110°)
¼ cup (½ stick) butter, softened to room temperature
¼ cup cooking oil
¾ cup sugar
1 egg

½ cup prepared mashed potatoes (use leftover or instant mashed potatoes if needed)
1½ tsp. salt
1 tsp. baking powder
½ tsp. baking soda
6 cups all purpose flour, divided
Melted butter (optional)

In a large bowl, dissolve the yeast in the warm water. Add the milk, butter, cooking oil, sugar, egg, and mashed potatoes and mix well. Stir in the salt, baking powder, baking soda, and half of the flour. Mix either by hand using a large wooden spoon or with an electric mixer, gradually adding flour until a soft dough is formed.

Turn out the dough onto a floured surface and knead it for about 8 minutes. Place the dough into a large greased bowl, turning the dough so the entire surface is greased. Cover the bowl and let the dough rise until doubled, about 1½ hours.

Punch down the dough. Turn it out onto a lightly floured surface and shape small amounts of dough to form approximately 32 round balls. Place the balls 2 inches apart on greased baking sheets. Cover the rolls and let them rise until doubled, about 30 to 45 minutes. Meanwhile, preheat the oven to 375°.

Bake for 15 to 18 minutes or until the tops are golden and the rolls are done. Remove them from the oven and, if desired, brush the tops with melted butter. Set the rolls on wire racks to cool.

Makes 32 rolls

Tip: *When making a large amount of rolls like this, it can be helpful to split the dough in half, and then in half again, continuing to halve the dough until you get the right number of rolls. In this case, you would split the dough into 2 even pieces, then 4, then 8, then 16, and finally end up with 32 uniform rolls.*

Oatmeal Rolls

¾ cup warm water (about 110°)
4½ tsp. (2 packages) active dry yeast
½ cup brown sugar
3 tsp. salt
2 cups rolled oats (you can use quick-cooking or old-fashioned)

½ cup shortening
2 cups milk
2 eggs, beaten
6 cups all-purpose flour, more or less

In a small bowl, add the warm water and then sprinkle the yeast on top. Let it stand for about 10 minutes.

In a large bowl, mix together the brown sugar, salt, and rolled oats. Cut in the shortening, using two forks, until the shortening is evenly distributed throughout the oatmeal mixture.

Scald the milk and pour it into the oat mixture, then cool it to lukewarm.

Add the beaten eggs, yeast mixture, and 1 cup of the flour to the bowl, then beat the batter until it is well mixed. Let it stand for about 15 minutes, until the batter is bubbly.

By hand, work in about 5 more cups of flour. Turn out the dough onto a floured work surface and knead it for 5 minutes.

Place the dough in a large greased bowl, turning the dough so the entire surface is greased. Cover the bowl and let the dough rise until it is doubled, about 1 to 1½ hours.

Shape the dough into balls, place them on greased baking sheets, cover the trays, and let the dough rise again until doubled, about 45 to 60 minutes. Meanwhile, preheat the oven to 400°.

Bake for 10 to 15 minutes or until done.

Makes 32 rolls

Overnight Refrigerator Butter Crescent Rolls

....

2¼ tsp. (1 package) active dry yeast	1 egg, beaten
2 T. warm water	2 tsp. salt
¼ cup sugar	5 to 6 cups all-purpose flour, divided
2 cups warm milk	½ cup (1 stick) butter, melted

In a large bowl, stir together the yeast, warm water, and sugar. When the yeast and sugar have dissolved, add the warm milk, egg, salt, and 2 cups of the flour. Mix the batter well, then add the melted butter and mix again. Next, add enough of the remaining flour to make a smooth dough. (It won't be quite as firm as you would need for a kneaded dough.) Do not knead. Instead, cover the bowl and let it sit in your refrigerator overnight so the dough has a chance to stiffen up enough to handle the next day.

Several hours before you want to bake the rolls, remove the bowl from the refrigerator, divide the dough into thirds, and turn out one piece of the dough onto a floured work surface. Roll the dough into a thin round, then cut each piece into 12 pie-shaped wedges. Roll up each wedge, from the outside to the center, into a crescent. Place them on a greased pan, being careful not to crowd the crescents. Repeat this process with the other two balls of dough. Cover the pans to let rolls rise until doubled, about 2 hours. (This can take a bit longer if the dough is very cold.)

Preheat the oven to 425° and bake the crescent rolls for 12 to 15 minutes or until baked through and very lightly browned.

Makes 36 rolls

Quick Caramel Rolls

TOPPING
½ cup brown sugar
½ cup (1 stick) butter, softened
2 T. light corn syrup

ROLLS
3 to 3½ cups all-purpose
  flour, divided
¼ cup sugar
1 tsp. salt
2¼ tsp. (1 package) active
  dry yeast
1 cup water
2 T. (¼ stick) butter
1 egg, beaten

FILLING
2 T. (¼ stick) butter, softened
¼ cup sugar
1 tsp. cinnamon

For the topping:

Grease a 9 x 13-inch baking pan or jelly roll pan. In a small bowl, mix together the topping ingredients, blending well. Drop by spoonfuls onto the prepared pan and spread evenly. Set aside.

For the rolls:

In a large bowl, whisk 1½ cups of the flour with the sugar, salt, and yeast.

In a small saucepan, heat the water and butter to about 125°. Pour the liquid into the flour mixture, add the beaten egg, and beat the batter for 3 minutes. Gradually stir in most of the remaining flour until the dough pulls away from the sides of the bowl.

Turn out the dough onto a floured work surface and knead it for 1 minute. Roll out the dough into a 15 x 7-inch rectangle and let it rest while you make the filling.

For the filling:

Evenly spread the butter over the dough. Make a mixture of the sugar and cinnamon and sprinkle it evenly over the buttered dough.

Starting with a 15-inch side, roll the dough into a tight log. Cut the log into 12 rounds and place the rounds on the prepared baking pan, cut side down. Cover the rolls and let them rise until doubled, about 45 minutes. Meanwhile, preheat the oven to 375°.

Bake for 25 to 30 minutes or until done. Allow the rolls to cool in the pan for one minute. Cover the baking pan with a serving platter and then carefully invert the two dishes together so the caramel underside of the rolls becomes the topping.

Makes 12 rolls

Rye Rolls

1 to 1¼ cups all-purpose flour, divided	1 cup milk
2 T. sugar	2 T. shortening
1 tsp. caraway seeds	1 egg
1 tsp. salt	1 cup rye flour
2¼ tsp. (1 package) active dry yeast	Melted butter for brushing

In a large bowl, whisk ¾ cup all-purpose flour with the sugar, caraway seeds, salt, and yeast.

In a small saucepan, heat the milk and shortening to 120° to 130°. Add the warm milk mixture and the egg to the flour mixture and stir to combine, then beat on medium speed for 3 minutes. Add the rye flour and beat well, then add enough of the remaining all-purpose flour to make a stiff batter.

Grease a muffin pan. Spoon the batter into the prepared muffin cups to ⅔ full and let the batter rise in a warm place, uncovered, for about 25 to 30 minutes. In the meantime, preheat the oven to 400°.

Bake the rolls for 12 to 15 minutes or until done. Brush the tops with melted butter while they are still warm.

Makes 10 to 12 rolls

Sticky Buns

¼ cup sugar	3 T. cooking oil
2¼ tsp. (1 package) active dry yeast	¼ cup water
1 tsp. salt	6 T. (¾ stick) butter, melted and cooled, divided
¼ tsp. baking soda	¾ cup brown sugar, divided
3 cups all-purpose flour, divided	¾ cup pecans, broken or chopped
1 cup buttermilk	1 tsp. cinnamon

In a large bowl, whisk the sugar, yeast, salt, and baking soda with 1 cup of the flour.

In a saucepan, heat the buttermilk and cooking oil over medium heat until warm (about 120°). Add the buttermilk mixture to the flour mixture and beat on high speed for 2 minutes. Using a wooden spoon, stir in 1½ cups of the remaining flour until the dough is smooth.

Lightly flour a clean work surface and turn out the dough. Knead it for about 8 minutes, adding more flour as needed to prevent the dough from sticking. Let the dough rest on the work surface while you are preparing the muffin pans.

In a small bowl, combine the water, 4 tablespoons of the melted butter, and ½ cup of the brown sugar. Distribute the mixture evenly among 12 muffin cups, then top with the pecans.

Roll out the dough into a 12 x 15-inch rectangle. Brush the dough with the remaining 2 tablespoons of melted butter. Combine the cinnamon with the remaining ¼ cup of brown sugar and sprinkle the cinnamon sugar evenly over the buttered dough.

Starting at a shorter end, roll up the dough into a log. (It will be about 12 inches long.) Cut it into 12 equal rounds and place them, cut side down, in the prepared muffin cups. Let the dough rise until doubled, about 1 to 1½ hours.

Preheat the oven to 350° and bake the buns for 25 minutes or until done. Remove the pans from the oven and immediately invert them onto serving plates, leaving the pans inverted over the rolls so the melted syrup and pecans have a chance to drip from the pan onto the rolls. Remove the pans and allow the sticky buns to cool for another 10 minutes before eating.

Makes 12 buns

Sweet Cream Buns

BUNS
1½ cups milk
¾ cup shortening
2¼ tsp. salt
¼ cup plus 1 T. sugar, divided
¾ cup warm water (about 115°)
3 T. (or use 3 packages) active dry yeast
3 eggs, beaten
7 cups all-purpose flour, more or less

FILLING
¼ cup shortening
½ cup milk
1 tsp. vanilla extract
3 cups powdered sugar

For the buns:

Scald the milk, then pour it into a large bowl and add the shortening, salt, and ¼ cup of the sugar. Stir to dissolve all ingredients, and then cool the mixture to lukewarm.

In a small bowl, add the warm water and 1 tablespoon sugar; stir until dissolved. Sprinkle the yeast on top and let it stand for 10 minutes.

Beat the yeast mixture with a fork and then stir it into the milk mixture. Add the beaten eggs and mix again.

Stir in 4 cups of the flour and beat the batter on medium speed for 3 minutes. By hand, work in just enough flour, about 3 more cups, to form a soft dough that pulls away from the sides of the bowl. Turn out the dough onto a floured work surface and knead for 5 to 6 minutes.

Place the dough in a greased bowl, turning the dough so the entire surface is greased. Cover the bowl and let the dough rise until doubled, about 1½ hours.

Punch down the dough, separate it into 48 equal pieces, and shape the pieces into balls. Place them on greased baking pans (jelly roll pans work well); cover the pans and let the rolls rise until doubled, about 1 hour.

Preheat the oven to 375° and bake for 25 minutes or until done.

For the filling:

Using an electric mixer on low speed, beat together the shortening, milk, and vanilla. Gradually add the powdered sugar, beating well after each addition. Continue beating until the filling is light and fluffy. Just before serving, cut a slit in each bun and fill with the filling.

Makes 48 buns

Baking bread is as much an art as it is a step-by-step procedure. When you are just starting out, following a recipe will give you a sense of confidence. But hopefully there will come a time when you decide to quit the careful measuring and begin to mix your loaves by feel. This is when your bread-baking skills will really shine, and you'll develop your own signature-style loaves.

Yeast breads are best made when you have several hours to devote to the process. Quick breads can be made in very little time and are a great choice for a last-minute addition to a meal or when unexpected guests show up. Both types of bread have their place in the family kitchen.

If you choose to use organic ingredients and grind your wheat and other grains, you can save a fair amount of money over store-bought loaves. Buying in bulk will increase your savings. Because most quick breads don't seem to have a store-bought equivalent, your loved ones will enjoy the special treat. If you are new to bread baking, without a doubt the easiest recipe in this section is the Buttermilk Whole Wheat Quick Bread. It has only 5 ingredients and very simple instructions! You'll be surprised how effortless it will be to produce an exceptionally tasty treat. And if you have several hours to devote to your baking, you can't go wrong with fresh yeast bread, such as Egg Bread (it's great for sandwiches!).

BREADS

Apple Bread

½ cup (1 stick) butter, room temperature
1 cup sugar
2 eggs
1 tsp. vanilla extract
2 cups all-purpose flour
1 T. baking soda
½ tsp. salt
⅓ cup sour milk (or ⅓ cup sour cream)
1 cup chopped apples
⅓ cup chopped walnuts

Preheat the oven to 350°.

In a large bowl, cream together the butter and sugar. Add the eggs and vanilla and beat well.

In another bowl, stir together the flour, baking soda, and salt. Alternately add the dry ingredients and the milk, half at a time, to the butter mixture, blending well after each addition. Stir in the apples and walnuts.

Pour the batter into a greased loaf pan and bake for 55 minutes or until done.

Serves 8

Banana Nut Bread

⅔ cup sugar
⅓ cup shortening
2 eggs
3 T. sour milk or buttermilk
1 cup mashed banana (slightly overripe bananas work best)
2 cups all-purpose flour
1 tsp. baking powder
½ tsp. baking soda
½ tsp. salt
½ cup chopped walnuts

Preheat the oven to 350°.

Using an electric mixer, cream together the sugar, shortening, and eggs. Stir in the sour milk and mashed bananas.

In another bowl, mix together the flour, baking powder, baking soda, and salt. Blend the dry ingredients into the banana mixture, then stir in the walnuts.

Pour the batter into a well-greased loaf pan. Let stand for 20 minutes, then bake for 50 to 60 minutes.

Serves 8

Basic Per Loaf Bread

For each loaf you wish to make, use the following measurements.

1 cup warm water, about 110° (or use half
   water, half milk)
1 tsp. melted shortening, butter, or vegetable oil
1 scant tsp. salt

1 T. honey, sugar, or other sweetener
1 tsp. active dry yeast (for 4 loaves, use
   1 rounded tablespoon)
3 cups all-purpose flour

In a mixing bowl, stir together the water, melted shortening, salt, and sugar. Sprinkle the yeast over the top of the mixture and let it stand until the yeast dissolves and starts bubbling a bit, about 10 minutes.

Stir in half of the flour (1½ cups flour for each loaf) and beat the batter until smooth. You can use an electric mixer for this part if desired, but you can also mix it by hand using a large wooden spoon. Add enough of the remaining flour to make a dough ball that holds together and comes away from the sides of the bowl.

Place the dough onto a floured work surface and knead well for 5 to 10 minutes, adding more flour as needed to keep the dough from sticking.

Put the dough into a large greased bowl and turn the dough to grease all the surfaces. Cover the bowl with a towel and let the dough rise until doubled, about 1 to 1½ hours.

Punch down the dough and then lightly knead it for a minute or so, grease all the surfaces once again, and let it rise in the greased bowl a second time until doubled. Punch down the dough and form it into a loaf (or however many loaves you've decided to make). Place the loaf seam side down into a greased loaf pan and let it rise until almost doubled, about 45 minutes.

Preheat the oven to 400°. Place the loaf in the preheated oven and then immediately turn the heat down to 350°. Bake about 30 minutes or until done. Remove the loaf from the oven, grease the top if desired (to help keep the top soft), take it out of the baking pan, and cool it on a wire rack.

Makes 1 loaf

When rising sourdough or yeast dough, the rising time will be affected by the ambient temperature. Cooler temperatures mean longer rising times, so take that into consideration when you are estimating what time the baked goods will be ready. I've found that 70 to 72 degrees works the best for me.

Basic Sourdough Bread

6⅓ cups unbleached all-purpose flour

1½ cups active sourdough starter

1⅔ cups water

3½ tsp. salt

In a large bowl, mix all the ingredients except the salt. Cover the bowl and let the dough sit at room temperature for about 30 minutes. Sprinkle the salt over the dough and mix it again to fully incorporate the salt throughout the dough. Keeping the dough in the container, stretch and fold the dough every 30 minutes or so, about 5 or 6 times, covering the bowl each time while the dough rests. Keeping the bowl covered, let the dough rise in the bowl until about doubled, usually 4 to 8 hours or overnight.

Gently turn out the dough onto a floured work surface and shape it into 1 or 2 loaves, then transfer the dough to a baking sheet. Cover the dough with plastic wrap so it doesn't dry out and let it rise for 2 to 4 hours or until almost doubled. Meanwhile, preheat the oven to 400° to 450° (a higher temperature will result in a darker crust).

Slash the top and bake the bread for 40 to 45 minutes or until done. Cool it on a wire rack.

Makes 1 large or 2 small loaves

Black Bread

1⅓ cups strong brewed coffee, cooled to
    about 110°
3 T. brown sugar
2½ tsp. active dry yeast
¼ cup cooking oil
¼ cup molasses

1 cup whole wheat flour
1 cup rye flour
2 T. unsweetened cocoa powder
1½ tsp. salt
2 cups all-purpose flour, more or less

In a medium bowl, mix together the coffee and brown sugar. Sprinkle the yeast on top of the mixture and let it stand until bubbly, about 10 minutes. Stir in the cooking oil and molasses.

In a large bowl, mix together the whole wheat flour, rye flour, cocoa powder, and salt. Add the yeast mixture and beat on medium (or beat by hand) for about 3 minutes. Gradually add the all-purpose flour, stirring to incorporate. When the dough ball begins to pull away from the sides of the bowl, turn it out onto a floured work surface and knead for about 8 minutes, adding more flour as needed to keep the dough from sticking.

Put the dough into a large greased bowl and turn it to grease all the surfaces of the dough as well. Cover the dough with a towel and let it rise until doubled, about 1½ to 2 hours. Keeping the dough in the bowl, punch it down and then lightly knead the dough for a minute or so. Grease all the surfaces once again, and let it rise in the greased bowl a second time until doubled, about 1 hour. Punch down the dough and form it into 12 round rolls. Place the rolls onto a greased baking sheet, cover them with a towel, and let them rise until almost doubled.

Preheat the oven to 375°, and then bake the rolls for 20 to 25 minutes or until done.

Makes 12 rounds

Buttermilk Whole Wheat Quick Bread

1 quart buttermilk
4 cups whole wheat flour
3 cups brown sugar
1 tsp. baking soda
Pinch of salt

Preheat the oven to 350°.

Combine all the ingredients and pour the batter into 2 greased loaf pans. Bake for 60 to 70 minutes.

Makes 2 loaves

If you grind your own wheat, the flour will always be fresh—no worries about it turning rancid. Also, wheat berries will store longer than wheat flour. The same goes for oat groats (used to make oatmeal) and other whole grains.

Carrot Nut Bread

....

1½ cups all-purpose flour	2 T. shortening, melted
1 cup whole wheat flour	1 cup warm milk
¾ cup brown sugar	2 eggs
2½ tsp. baking powder	1 cup carrot, peeled and grated
1 tsp. baking soda	½ cup nuts, chopped
1 tsp. salt	

Preheat the oven to 375°.

In a medium bowl, whisk together the all-purpose flour, whole wheat flour, brown sugar, baking powder, baking soda, and salt; set aside.

In a large bowl, whisk the shortening, milk, and eggs. Add the flour mixture to the liquid mixture and stir to combine. Fold in the carrots and nuts.

Bake in a greased loaf pan for 50 to 60 minutes or until done. Allow the bread to cool before slicing.

Makes 1 loaf

Chocolate Zucchini Bread

3 eggs, beaten
1 cup cooking oil
1¾ cups sugar
1 T. vanilla extract
2 cups grated zucchini
3 cups all-purpose flour (or use half whole
   wheat and half all-purpose)

½ cup unsweetened cocoa
1 tsp. salt
1 tsp. baking soda
1 tsp. baking powder
½ cup chopped walnuts or pecans (optional)

Preheat the oven to 350°.

In a large bowl, combine the eggs, oil, sugar, and vanilla, then stir in the zucchini.

In a separate bowl, combine the flour, cocoa, salt, baking soda, and baking powder. Add the flour mixture to the zucchini mixture and blend well. Add the nuts, if using, and stir again.

Grease and flour 2 loaf pans and pour the batter into the pans.

Bake for 45 minutes. Cool the bread in the pans for 10 to 15 minutes, then remove the loaves to a wire rack to finish cooling.

Makes 2 loaves

Egg Bread

1½ cups milk, scalded	4½ tsp. (2 packages) active dry yeast
½ cup (1 stick) butter	2 eggs, beaten
½ cup plus ½ tsp. sugar, divided	9 cups all-purpose flour, more or less
½ cup warm water (110°)	2 tsp. salt

In a large mixing bowl, pour the scalded milk over the butter and ½ cup of the sugar. Allow the mixture to cool while you prepare the yeast.

In a small bowl, stir the final ½ teaspoon sugar into the warm water and then stir in the yeast. Let it stand for 5 minutes.

Add the yeast mixture to the cooled milk mixture and stir. Alternately add the eggs and 3 cups of the flour. Add the salt and beat the dough for 3 minutes. By hand, continue adding the final 3 cups of flour, and knead the dough for 8 to 10 minutes. Place the dough in a greased bowl, turning the dough so the entire surface is greased. Cover the bowl and let the dough rise until doubled, about 1 to 1½ hours.

Shape the dough into 3 loaves and place it into greased loaf pans. Let it rise, uncovered, until the dough is about one inch above the tops of the loaf pans.

Preheat the oven to 425°. Bake the bread for 10 minutes; then reduce the temperature to 350° and bake for an additional 30 to 40 minutes.

Makes 3 loaves

Good-for-You Bread

3½ to 4 cups all-purpose flour	⅔ cup honey
1¾ cups rye flour	3 T. butter
1¾ cups whole wheat flour	2 T. molasses
2 tsp. salt	½ cup shelled sunflower seeds
6¾ tsp. (3 packages) active dry yeast	¼ cup wheat germ
1¾ cups milk	¼ cup whole bran cereal
¾ cup water	

In a large bowl, combine 2 cups of the all-purpose flour with the rye and whole wheat flours.

In another large bowl, measure out 3 cups of the flour mixture and add the salt and yeast.

In a small saucepan, heat together the milk, water, honey, butter, and molasses to 120° to 130°. Add the warmed milk mixture to the 3 cups of flour, salt, and yeast. With an electric mixer or a large wooden spoon, beat the dough for about 3 minutes. Stir in the sunflower seeds, wheat germ, bran cereal, the remaining flour mixture, and most of the remaining all-purpose flour, until the dough begins to form a ball and leaves the sides of the bowl.

Turn out the dough onto a floured work surface and knead it for about 10 minutes, adding more of the all-purpose flour as needed. Place the dough into a greased bowl, turning the dough so the entire surface is greased, and cover with a towel. Let it rise in a warm place until doubled in size, about 1 to 1½ hours.

Punch down the dough, divide it in half, shape each half into a ball, and allow it to rest on the counter, covered, for 15 minutes.

Shape the dough balls into 2 loaves and place them into 2 greased loaf pans. Cover the pans and let the dough rise again until it is almost doubled, about 30 to 45 minutes.

Preheat the oven to 350° and bake the loaves for 40 to 45 minutes or until done. Remove the bread from the loaf pans and cool on a wire rack.

Makes 2 loaves

Herb Bubble Bread

1 cup milk, scalded and cooled to about 110°	½ cup Parmesan cheese
1 T. sugar	¾ tsp. dried parsley flakes
1 tsp. salt	¼ tsp. dill weed
4½ tsp. (2 packages) active dry yeast	⅛ tsp. each dried thyme, basil, and rosemary
2 eggs, beaten	½ cup (1 stick) butter, melted
4½ cups all-purpose flour	2 tsp. minced garlic

Mix together the milk, sugar, and salt. Add the yeast, eggs, and most of the flour. Turn out the dough onto a floured surface and knead for 8 minutes, adding more flour as needed so the dough doesn't stick. Place the dough in a greased bowl, turning it so the entire surface is greased. Cover the bowl and let the dough rise until doubled, about 1 to 1½ hours. Punch the dough down and let it rise until doubled again, about an hour. Punch it down and let it rest for 10 minutes.

Meanwhile, in a small bowl, mix together the Parmesan cheese, parsley flakes, dill weed, thyme, basil, and rosemary. In another small bowl, mix together the melted butter and minced garlic.

Roll the dough into balls the size of a walnut; roll them in the melted garlic butter and then the herb mixture and place them in a greased angel food cake pan in staggered rows. Cover and let rise for 1 hour. Meanwhile, preheat the oven to 350°.

Bake for 22 to 26 minutes or until done. Cool the bread for 10 minutes then remove from the pan to a wire rack. Serve warm.

Makes 1 round loaf

Honey Corn Bread

1 cup cornmeal
1 cup all-purpose flour
1 T. baking powder
½ tsp. salt

1 cup buttermilk
1 egg
¼ cup (½ stick) butter, melted
½ cup honey

Preheat the oven to 425°.

In a large bowl, mix together the cornmeal, flour, baking powder, and salt.

In a medium bowl, whisk together the buttermilk, egg, and melted butter until well blended. Add the honey and whisk again to mix well. Add the buttermilk mixture to the cornmeal mixture and mix by hand; don't overmix. (The batter will be lumpy.)

Grease or butter an 8 x 8-inch or 9 x 9-inch baking dish and pour the batter into the prepared pan. Bake for 20 to 25 minutes or until done.

Makes 1 loaf

Lemon Tea Bread

BREAD
⅓ cup shortening
1 cup sugar
2 eggs, well beaten
2 cups all-purpose flour
1 tsp. baking powder
⅛ tsp. salt
½ cup milk
2 tsp. lemon juice
1 tsp. grated lemon rind
½ cup walnuts

GLAZE
2 tsp. sugar
2 tsp. grated lemon rind
1 tsp. lemon juice

For the bread:

In a large bowl, cream together the shortening and sugar, mixing well. Add the eggs and beat well again.

In another bowl, combine 1 cup of the flour with the baking powder and salt and then add the dry ingredients to the shortening mixture. Blend well to incorporate, then blend in the milk, lemon juice, lemon rind, and walnuts. Add the remaining cup of flour and mix again. Pour the batter into a well-greased loaf pan and bake for 90 minutes at 300°.

For the glaze:

Mix together the sugar, lemon rind, and lemon juice. (Add a few more drops of lemon juice if the mixture is too thick.) Spread the glaze on top of the baked loaf and then let it cool.

Makes 1 loaf

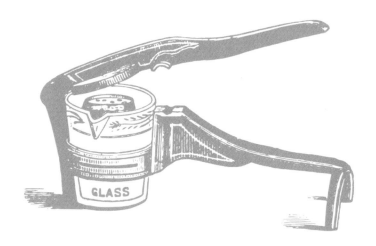

No-Knead Oatmeal Bread

2 to 2½ cups all-purpose flour, divided	1 cup water
¾ cup rolled oats	¼ cup molasses
1 tsp. salt	¼ cup (½ stick) butter
2¼ tsp. (1 package) active dry yeast	1 egg

In a large bowl, combine 1 cup of the flour with the rolled oats, salt, and yeast; blend well.

In a small saucepan, heat the water, molasses, and butter to quite warm (120° to 130°). Add the warm liquid and the egg to the flour mixture. Using an electric mixer, blend at low speed until the flour is incorporated, then turn the mixer to medium speed and continue mixing for 3 minutes. Stir in an additional 1 to 1½ cups of the flour to form a stiff batter. Cover the bowl with a towel and let the batter rise in a warm place until doubled, about 45 to 60 minutes.

Stir down the batter and then pour it into a greased loaf pan. Cover the pan and let the dough rise until the batter reaches the top of the pan, about 30 minutes, although you'll want to watch it carefully so it doesn't rise too high. Meanwhile, preheat the oven to 350°.

Bake for 35 to 40 minutes or until done. Remove the bread from the pan immediately and cool it on a wire rack.

Makes 1 loaf

Pumpkin Whole Wheat Quick Bread

5 cups whole wheat flour	½ tsp. cloves
3 cups brown sugar	2½ cups canned pumpkin
1 heaping T. baking soda	1 cup cooking oil
1 tsp. salt	2 eggs
1 tsp. cinnamon	

In a large bowl, use a large wooden spoon to combine the flour, brown sugar, baking soda, salt, cinnamon, and cloves. Add the canned pumpkin, oil, and eggs and mix again. When the batter is thoroughly blended, divide it between 2 greased loaf pans.

Bake at 350° for about 1 hour and 20 minutes or until done.

Makes 2 loaves

Quick Garlic Cheese Breadsticks

½ cup (1 stick) butter, melted
2½ cups all-purpose flour
4 tsp. baking powder
1⅓ cups milk

2 tsp. garlic powder
Parmesan cheese to taste
Dried parsley (optional)

Preheat the oven to 450°.

Pour the melted butter into a 9 x 13-inch baking pan. In a large mixing bowl, stir together the flour and baking powder, then pour in the milk and stir until a soft dough forms. Knead the dough for about 3 minutes, adding extra flour if the dough is too sticky.

On a floured work surface, roll out the dough to form a rectangle that is roughly 8 x 11 inches and ½ inch thick. Cut the dough into 6 to 8 strips that are about 1½ inches wide. Place the strips into the pan and turn them so both sides are buttered. Sprinkle the strips with the garlic powder, Parmesan cheese, and parsley.

Bake for 15 to 20 minutes or until done.

Makes 6 to 8 breadsticks

Rustic Peasant Bread

2¼ tsp. (1 package) active dry yeast
1 T. sugar
2 tsp. salt
2 cups warm water (about 110°)

1 T. oil, plus more for brushing the top of the loaf
  (olive oil tastes great in this recipe)
4½ cups all-purpose flour

In a large bowl, combine the yeast, sugar, and salt; add the warm water and stir together, then add the oil and stir again. Add the flour a cup at a time, incorporating it well after each addition. Once all the flour is added, knead the dough until it is smooth, about 5 to 7 minutes. Place the dough in a greased bowl and turn it to grease all sides of the dough. Cover the bowl and let the dough rise for 30 minutes.

Form the dough into a round loaf and place it on a greased cookie sheet. Cover the dough and let it rise again, about 45 minutes. Meanwhile, preheat the oven to 425°.

Brush the top of the loaf with oil, then bake at 425° for 10 minutes. Reduce the heat to 375° and brush again with oil, then continue baking for 20 more minutes.

Makes 1 round loaf

Rye and Dill Bread

3½ to 4 cups all-purpose flour
1½ cups rye flour
½ cup instant milk powder
4½ tsp. (2 packages) active
  dry yeast

2 tsp. sugar
1 tsp. salt
1 tsp. caraway seeds
1 tsp. dill seeds

1 tsp. dill weed
2¾ cups water
2 tsp. shortening

In a large bowl, combine 2 cups of the all-purpose flour with the rye flour, milk powder, yeast, sugar, salt, caraway seeds, dill seeds, and dill weed.

In a saucepan, heat the water and shortening until the shortening melts and the mixture reaches 120° to 130°. Add the warm liquid to the flour mixture and then beat for 3 minutes. Stir in enough remaining all-purpose flour to form a soft dough that pulls away from the sides of the bowl.

Turn out the dough onto a floured work surface and knead for 8 minutes. Place the dough into a greased bowl, turning the dough so the entire surface is greased. Cover the bowl and let the dough rise until doubled, about 1 hour.

Punch down the dough and let it rest on a lightly floured surface, covered, for about 10 minutes. Divide the dough in half and form 2 round loaves. Place the loaves onto 2 greased baking sheets, cover, and let the dough rise again for about 35 to 45 minutes. Meanwhile, preheat the oven to 375°.

Before baking, use a sharp knife to make 3 shallow slashes across the top of each loaf. Bake for 30 to 35 minutes or until done, exchanging the positions of the pans halfway through the baking time.

Makes 2 round loaves

Soy Flour Bread

2¼ tsp. (1 package) active dry yeast	1 T. shortening
½ cup warm water (about 120°)	1 tsp. salt
1 T. plus one pinch sugar	2 cups soy flour
2 cups warm milk or water (about 120°)	4 cups all-purpose flour, plus more for kneading

In a small bowl, dissolve the yeast and a pinch of sugar in the warm water. Let it stand for about 10 minutes or until bubbly.

In a large bowl, stir together the warm milk, shortening, salt, and the tablespoon of sugar. Add the yeast mixture and then gradually add the soy flour, mixing as you go. Once all the soy flour is added, beat the dough for about 2 to 3 minutes. Gradually add the all-purpose flour (you'll probably need to use a large wooden spoon when the dough gets thick) until it forms a loose ball and pulls away from the sides of the bowl. Turn out the dough onto a floured work surface and knead it until smooth and elastic, about 8 minutes.

Place the ball of dough into a large greased bowl, turning the dough so the entire surface is greased. Cover the bowl and set it in a warm place to let the dough rise until doubled, about 2 hours.

Divide the dough in half and shape it into 2 loaves. Place the loaves in greased loaf pans, loosely cover the pans, and let the dough rise until it reaches about an inch above the top of each pan, about 45 minutes. Meanwhile, preheat the oven to 375°.

Bake the bread for 35 to 40 minutes or until done.

Makes 2 loaves

Buttermilk Soda Bread

3¾ cups all-purpose flour (or use half all-purpose and half whole wheat flour) plus a bit more for kneading	1½ tsp. baking soda
	1½ tsp. salt
	2 cups buttermilk

Preheat the oven to 425°.

Line a cookie sheet with parchment paper or a silicone baking mat and set it aside for now.

In a large mixing bowl, whisk together the flour, baking soda, and salt. Make a shallow well in the center of the flour and then add the buttermilk, stirring until the dough begins to come together.

Tip out the ball of dough onto a floured work surface (it will be loose and shaggy) and gently knead the dough 8 to 10 times.

Transfer the dough onto the prepared baking sheet, and then pat the dough into a flat circle about 1 or 2 inches high. Use a sharp knife to score the top into a cross shape about ¼-inch deep.

Immediately place the bread in the oven and bake for 20 minutes. Turn down the heat to 375° and bake for another 20 minutes or until the bread is golden brown and there's a hollow sound when the bottom of the loaf is thumped.

Transfer the bread to a wire rack to cool for about 30 minutes before slicing.

Makes 1 loaf

When you think of homemade soup, you probably envision old-fashioned chicken noodle. While this tried-and-true recipe hits the spot, there are so many options to explore beyond this classic.

Soup is easily underestimated. It can do far more than comfort a person with a cold. Soup can take center stage as a meal—check out the Curry Lentil—or it can complement almost any entrée. As seasonings and main ingredients are cooked and stirred together, a new and delicious creation is born. The possibilities truly are endless.

Among these 20 recipes, I'm confident you can find some new family favorites. I hope you'll give them a try.

Beef and Green Bean Soup

4 cups beef broth
1 cup cooked beef, cubed
2 potatoes, peeled and diced
2 carrots, peeled and thinly sliced
1 stalk celery, thinly sliced
1 small onion, diced

¼ to ½ tsp. thyme
¼ to ½ tsp. rosemary
1 can (about 15 oz.) green beans (I use a 1-pint or
    1½-pint jar of home-canned green beans)
1 cup whipping cream or evaporated milk
Salt and pepper to taste

In a large pot, bring the beef broth to a boil. Add the beef, potatoes, carrots, celery, onion, thyme, and rosemary. Reduce the heat and simmer, covered, for about 30 minutes or until the vegetables are tender. Add the green beans and taste the broth, then add salt and pepper to taste. Continue to simmer for 5 to 10 minutes or more. Just before serving, lower the heat and stir in the cream; heat thoroughly but do not boil.

Serves 4 to 6

Cabbage and Apple Soup

2½ cups chicken broth
2½ cups water
1 (8 oz.) can tomato sauce
2 tsp. lemon juice
3 cups cabbage
2 cups apple, peeled, cored, and diced

¼ cup onion, diced
1 T. caraway seeds
1 clove garlic, crushed, or ¼ tsp. garlic powder
Pinch of sugar
Salt and pepper to taste

In a large pot, combine the chicken broth, water, tomato sauce, and lemon juice. Stir well to mix, then bring the broth to a boil. Stir in the remaining ingredients and lower the heat to a simmer. Continue simmering for about 30 minutes, stirring occasionally, until the apples and cabbage are tender. Before you serve the soup, taste the broth and adjust the seasonings if needed.

The apples make a surprising addition to this delicious side dish or lunch. For an even heartier meal, you can brown a bit of ground beef, drain off the fat, and add the beef to the soup.

Serves 6 to 8

Cabbage, Bean, and Ham Soup

2½ cups cabbage, coarsely chopped or shredded
2 (15 oz.) cans navy beans, drained, rinsed,
   and drained again
1 cup cooked ham, chopped
1 cup onion, diced
2 carrots, peeled and thickly sliced

1 cup turnip, peeled and chopped
   (about 1 medium-sized turnip)
1 tsp. marjoram
¼ tsp. pepper
1 bay leaf
6 cups water
Salt and pepper to taste

In a large soup pot, add all the ingredients and stir to mix. Bring the soup to a boil and then lower the heat, cover the pot, and simmer until the vegetables are tender. Taste the broth and adjust the seasonings as necessary (the amount of salt you need will depend on what kind of ham you use). Before serving, discard the bay leaf.

Serves 6 to 8

Cheddar Cheese Soup with Pumpernickel Croutons

4 slices pumpernickel bread, cut into cubes
¼ cup butter, plus more for the croutons, if desired
1 medium onion, finely diced
¼ cup flour

3 cups chicken broth
3 cups milk
4 cups shredded cheddar cheese
Salt and pepper to taste

To make the croutons, place the bread cubes on a cookie sheet and set them in a 200° oven to let them dry out and get a bit crisp. If desired, you can also butter the bread before baking the cubes. This is tasty but not necessary. Check them every 10 minutes or so and stir them so all sides are exposed. When the croutons are done to your liking, you can turn the oven off, crack the oven door open, and leave them inside to stay warm. Alternatively, you can remove them from the oven and when they're cooled down, place them in a serving dish.

While the croutons are baking, melt the butter in a soup pot over medium heat, add the onion, and cook until the onion is soft and translucent. Add the flour and stir constantly to thoroughly mix the flour with the onions. Gradually add the chicken broth and cook, still stirring constantly, until the mixture has thickened slightly. Add the milk and continue to stir until the soup is very hot—just under the boiling point. Turn off the heat and add the cheddar cheese; stir until the cheese is completely melted. (You may need to turn the stove back on at low heat for a bit if you have trouble getting all the cheese to melt.) Add salt and pepper to taste.

Remove the pumpernickel croutons from the oven if you haven't already done so, and place them in a serving bowl to bring to the table. Ladle the soup into individual bowls and serve with some of the croutons sprinkled on top.

Serves 4 to 6

Chicken Broth with Soda Cracker Dumplings

1 egg
2 T. butter, melted and cooled slightly
6 T. finely crushed soda crackers (such as Saltines)
1 T. milk
¼ tsp. parsley

1 tsp. finely minced onion
¼ tsp. celery salt
Dash of pepper
2 quarts chicken broth

For the dumplings:

Beat the egg well in a medium mixing bowl. Stir in the melted butter. Add the remaining ingredients—except the broth—and mix well. Using your hands, shape the cracker mixture into dumplings that are about the size of a small, unshelled walnut, squeezing the dumplings so the mixture sticks together well. Lay them out on a plate or towel for 30 minutes to give them time to meld. (As the dumplings sit, the cracker crumbs will become saturated by the liquids and swell slightly.)

For the soup:

Pour the broth into a large pot and bring it to a simmer. Drop the cracker dumplings into the broth and immediately reduce the heat to medium-low. Cover the pot and cook the dumplings for 10 minutes without lifting the lid. Serve immediately.

Serves 6 to 8

Even inside city limits, many towns allow you to keep a few chickens (though often not roosters because they're noisy). Chickens are easy to maintain, their composted droppings make for excellent garden fertilizer, and the quality and taste of the eggs are totally worth the small outlay of money and effort.

Chicken Chowder with Mushrooms

¾ lb. boneless, skinless chicken, cut into
    bite-size pieces
2½ cups chicken broth
3 carrots, peeled and diced
2 stalks celery, chopped
1 small onion, diced
½ cup fresh mushrooms, sliced (I use
    button mushrooms)

½ tsp. parsley
¼ tsp. rosemary
1 T. butter
3 T. flour
1 cup milk
1 cup peas (fresh or frozen)
Salt and pepper to taste

In a large soup pot, add the chicken and broth, bring the broth to a boil, and simmer until the chicken is cooked through. Because the pieces of chicken are small, this won't take more than about 5 to 10 minutes. Using a slotted spoon, remove the cooked chicken and set it aside for now.

Add the carrots, celery, onion, mushrooms, parsley, and rosemary to the pot and return the broth to a boil. Lower the heat, cover the pot, and simmer the soup until the vegetables are tender, about 12 minutes.

Using the slotted spoon, transfer about half of the cooked vegetables to a food processor or blender and puree. Return the pureed vegetables and the cooked chicken to the soup pot and keep the heat on fairly low; you don't want the soup to boil, but you do want it to be hot.

In a small saucepan, melt the butter and add the flour, stirring constantly. Cook and stir for about 30 seconds and then—still stirring constantly—gradually add the milk. Cook until the mixture thickens and then add it to the soup, along with the peas. Simmer for several minutes more until the peas are hot. If you use frozen peas, you'll have to simmer the soup for a bit longer.

Before serving, add salt and pepper to taste.

Serves 4

Corn and Clam Chowder

2 slices bacon, cut into small pieces
3 potatoes, peeled and cut into bite-size pieces
¾ cup onion, diced
½ cup celery, diced
2 cups milk
2 (6½ oz.) cans minced clams, drained
   with liquid reserved

¾ tsp. thyme
⅛ tsp. pepper
1 (15 oz.) can or 1 pint jar homemade creamed corn
1 (11 oz.) can or 1 pint jar home-canned
   corn, drained

In a large pot, cook the bacon until it is brown and crisp. Use a slotted spoon to transfer the cooked bacon onto paper towels.

Add the potatoes, onion, and celery to the bacon drippings in the pot and cook, gently stirring (so the veggies don't stick to the bottom) for 5 minutes. Add the milk, reserved clam juice, thyme, and pepper. Mix well, reduce the heat to medium-low, cover the pot, and simmer for about 20 minutes or until the potatoes are tender.

Take 2 cups of the vegetable mixture and puree it until smooth, using either a food processor or a blender. Return the pureed vegetables to the soup pot and then add the creamed corn, regular corn, and clams. Return the soup to a boil and then reduce the heat and simmer until the soup is completely hot, about 5 minutes.

To serve, ladle the soup into individual bowls and sprinkle some of the cooked bacon on the top of each serving. (Alternatively, you can simply add the bacon to the soup pot and stir to mix before ladling the soup into individual bowls.)

Serves 4

Creamy Carrot and Rice Soup

4 to 5 carrots, peeled and grated
1 onion, peeled and minced
4 cups chicken or vegetable broth
1 cup cooked rice
3 T. butter

1 tsp. salt
1 T. sugar
1 cup milk
Powdered ginger and turmeric (optional)

In a pot over medium-high heat, add the carrots and onion with enough water to cover them. Cook for a few minutes until they are soft. (It won't take long.) Drain off the water, then add the broth, cooked rice, butter, salt, and sugar and continue cooking. When the soup is heated evenly, add the milk and continue to heat on low until the soup is hot enough to serve.

Option: You can puree some or all of this soup if you like it creamy and smooth. I also sometimes add a bit of powdered ginger or turmeric for extra flavor and color, but it's good as it is.

Serves 4

Curried Lentil Soup

5 cups water or vegetable broth
1 cup lentils, rinsed and picked over
1 onion, diced
2 stalks celery, diced
2 carrots, peeled and diced

1 (15 oz.) can tomato sauce
½ to ¾ tsp. curry powder
½ tsp. basil
Salt and pepper to taste

Combine all ingredients in a large pot and simmer for 1 to 2 hours. Adjust the seasonings to taste and serve warm.

Serves 5 to 6

Egg Soup

....

6 cups chicken broth	3 T. lemon juice
¼ cup uncooked white rice	3 eggs, hard-boiled, peeled, and diced
4 eggs, raw	

In a soup pot, heat the broth and rice to boiling. Reduce the heat to low, cover the pot, and cook the soup for about 20 minutes or until the rice is cooked.

In a medium mixing bowl, add the eggs and lemon and use a hand beater or a whisk to beat the mixture until it is frothy.

Reduce the heat for the soup to the lowest setting. Stir a small amount of the hot broth into the egg mixture and then, stirring constantly, pour the egg mixture into the pot of simmering soup. Continue to stir constantly until the soup is heated through but not boiling. Just before serving, taste and add salt or pepper if needed.

Ladle the soup into individual bowls and sprinkle hard-boiled eggs on top.

Serves 4 to 6

Leek and Potato Soup

....

3 to 4 good-sized leeks	½ scant tsp. pepper
2 T. butter	¼ tsp. marjoram
4 cups chicken or vegetable broth	½ tsp. thyme
2 lbs. potatoes, peeled and diced	1 bay leaf
1 tsp. salt	½ cup heavy cream or half-and-half

Cut the leeks lengthwise in half or quarters (depending on their size) and then rinse them well to get rid of any sand or soil still clinging to the interior surfaces. Using only the white and light-green portions, thinly chop the leeks.

In a heavy soup pot, melt the butter over low heat; add the chopped leeks, cover the pot, and cook on low for about 10 minutes or until the leeks are softened but not browned. Occasionally remove the lid and stir the leeks gently to check for browning.

Add the broth, potatoes, salt, pepper, marjoram, thyme, and the bay leaf. Simmer the soup for 20 minutes, stirring occasionally, until the potatoes are soft. Using a potato masher or ricer, mash the soup to break up some of the potatoes and make a creamier soup. You can mash more or less depending on how chunky you like your soup. Add the cream and increase the heat but do not allow it to boil. Taste the soup and add more salt and pepper if desired.

Ladle the soup into individual bowls and eat it plain or garnish with croutons, a dollop of sour cream, or shredded Parmesan or cheddar cheese.

Serves 6

Meatball Soup

MEATBALLS	SOUP
2 lbs. ground beef	1 or 2 T. oil
2 tsp. salt	2 small or 1 large onion, diced
⅛ tsp. pepper	2 cups celery, diced
2 eggs, beaten	4 cups potatoes, peeled and diced
¼ cup chopped fresh parsley (or 1 T. dried parsley flakes)	¼ cup uncooked white rice
	6 cups tomato juice or V8 juice
½ cup crushed cracker crumbs or bread crumbs	6 cups water
	1 T. sugar
2 T. milk	1 tsp. salt
5 T. flour	1½ cups frozen corn, or a mixture of corn and peas (you can also use fresh)

Combine the first 7 meatball ingredients in a large bowl and mix them together thoroughly. Form meat balls that are about the size of walnuts, and then dredge them in the flour.

In a large soup pot, heat the oil over medium heat and add the meatballs. Brown them on all sides, then add the remaining soup ingredients except the corn. Bring the mixture to a boil, reduce the heat, cover with a tight-fitting lid, and continue to cook until the vegetables and rice are tender, about 20 minutes. Add the corn last and cook for about 10 minutes more.

Serves 12 to 15

Old-Fashioned Chicken Noodle Soup

1 (3 to 4 lb.) chicken	Salt, pepper, and other herbs to taste
1 stalk celery, chunked into thirds	4 cups cooked noodles (about 8 oz. uncooked), drained
1 small onion, quartered	
2 carrots, peeled and chopped or sliced	

In a large pot, add the chicken, celery, and onion; cover with water to about 3 inches above the chicken. Cover the pot, bring the water to a boil, and then lower the heat to keep a slow simmer going. Cook until the chicken is done, about 1½ hours. Remove the chicken from the pot and let it cool. Strain the vegetables out of the broth and then return the broth to the soup pot; allow it to cool enough so that the fat rises to the top, and then skim off as much fat as you can.

Turn the heat to about medium and return the broth to a simmer. Prepare the carrots and add them to the broth. Cook them until they are soft.

In the meantime, remove the chicken meat from the bones and skin. Chop or shred the chicken into bite-size pieces and add the meat to the soup. At this point, taste the soup and add salt, pepper, and any other spices that sound good to you, such as thyme, summer savory, marjoram, or oregano. When the carrots are done, add the cooked noodles and continue to simmer for several minutes to heat thoroughly.

Serves 10

Old-Fashioned Vegetable Beef Soup

¼ cup vegetable oil
1 small onion, diced
3 stalks celery, sliced
2 carrots, peeled and sliced
½ small head cabbage, coarsely shredded
1 zucchini, chopped
1½ lbs. beef stew meat, cut into bite-size pieces
6 medium (or 4 large) potatoes, peeled and diced
2 (14½ oz.) cans diced tomatoes, undrained
    or 1 quart home-canned tomatoes

6 cups water
1 (16 oz.) can cut green beans (don't use
    French-style) or 1 pint jar home-canned
    green beans, drained
1 (8 oz.) can baby lima beans, drained
4 tsp. salt
⅓ tsp. pepper
½ tsp. basil

In a heavy-bottomed soup pot, add the oil, onion, celery, carrots, cabbage, and zucchini, and cook until the vegetables are lightly browned. With a slotted spoon, remove the vegetables to a large bowl and set them aside for now.

In the same pot, use what is left of the oil to cook the beef cubes, stirring frequently, until all the pieces are well browned on all sides. Add the reserved cooked vegetables and all the other ingredients and heat to boiling. Reduce the heat to low, cover the pot, and simmer the soup for about 30 minutes or until the meat and potatoes are tender.

Serves 8

Note: *If you are cooking for those who don't love lima beans, you can substitute a cup of frozen peas, only adding them during the last few minutes of cooking. This is a beautiful—and versatile—soup.*

Quick and Easy Tomato Soup

2 (6 oz.) cans tomato paste
2 quarts water
2 stalks celery, chunked into thirds
1 T. sugar
1 tsp. salt (go easy on the salt; you can always
    add more later)
¼ tsp. each oregano, basil, thyme, rosemary,
    onion powder, and celery seed

⅛ tsp. garlic powder
1 T. sugar
Pepper to taste
1 bay leaf (optional, but good)
¼ to ⅓ cup milk, half-and-half, or heavy cream
1 T. butter
1 T. flour

In a large pot, combine all the ingredients up to the milk; stir to mix well. Bring the liquid to a boil and then turn the heat down to simmer for 20 minutes. Remove the celery pieces and bay leaf. Taste the broth and adjust the seasonings if needed.

Melt 1 tablespoon of butter in a small saucepan, then whisk in 1 tablespoon of flour to form a roux. Stirring constantly, gradually add about 1 cup of the tomato soup to the roux. Keep stirring while you wait for the mixture to thicken, and when it does, stir the mixture into the soup pot.

Continue stirring as you add the milk, and heat until the soup is hot but not boiling.

Serves 6 to 8

Spaghetti Soup

1 lb. ground beef
½ cup onion, chopped
½ cup bell pepper, chopped
1 stalk celery, chopped
1 carrot, peeled and chopped
2 cloves garlic, minced
2 (14½ oz.) cans diced tomatoes, undrained
1 (15 oz.) can tomato sauce plus half of the can of water (this helps to get every last bit of tomato sauce)

2½ cups water
1 T. sugar
1 tsp. Italian seasoning
½ tsp. salt
¼ tsp. pepper
2 oz. uncooked spaghetti noodles, broken into small pieces (see note below)
Parmesan cheese for topping

In a large pot, add the ground beef, onion, bell pepper, celery, carrot, and garlic; brown the mixture until the ground beef is no longer pink, then drain off the fat.

Add the undrained diced tomatoes, tomato sauce, water, sugar, Italian seasoning, salt, and pepper and bring to a boil. Add the noodles, return the soup to a boil, reduce heat, and simmer until the noodles are done, about 12 minutes. Taste the broth and adjust the seasonings if needed. At the table, let everyone add as much or as little Parmesan cheese as they desire.

Serves 8

Note: *You don't need to weigh the spaghetti noodles. Just grab a handful that is about 2¼ inches in circumference (about ¾-inch in diameter).*

Split Pea Soup

1 cup dried split peas
12 cups water, divided
1 ham hock or pieces of cubed ham
1 carrot, peeled and finely diced
1 onion, finely diced

1 potato, peeled and finely diced
¼ cup celery, finely diced
¼ cup green bell pepper, finely diced (optional)
Salt and pepper to taste

In a large pot, boil 6 cups of water and then add the dried peas. Turn off the heat, cover the pot, and let the peas soak for 1 hour. Drain the water from the peas and add 6 cups of fresh water and the remaining ingredients. Bring the water to a boil and then lower the heat to a simmer. Continue cooking until the peas are tender (about 45 minutes, depending on how old the peas are). You will need to add more water during this cooking time because the split peas absorb water as they cook.

Serves 4 to 6

Note: *You can make split pea soup (using this recipe) without soaking the peas first, but the soup will take longer to cook until the peas are tender—about 2 hours.*

Sweet Potato and Tortilla Chip Soup

1 T. vegetable oil
1 cup onion, chopped
2 cloves garlic, minced
4 sweet potatoes, peeled and cut into ½-inch
   cubes (4 cups total)
3 cups chicken broth
½ tsp. cumin
½ tsp. oregano
½ tsp. chili powder

¼ tsp. red pepper flakes or ground red pepper
   (use less if you don't like a lot of heat)
1 (14½ oz.) can diced tomatoes, including juice,
   or 1 pint jar home-canned tomatoes
1 cup fresh or frozen corn
1 (4½ oz.) can chopped green chilies
3 T. chopped fresh cilantro or parsley
Tortilla chips, broken but not crushed

In a large pot, heat the oil and then add the onion and garlic. Cook, stirring occasionally, until the onion is tender and translucent.

Stir in the sweet potatoes, broth, cumin, oregano, chili powder, and red pepper. Bring the soup to a boil and then reduce the heat to low and simmer, covered, for about 20 minutes or until the sweet potatoes are tender.

Transfer about 2 cups of soup (more if you prefer a creamier soup) to a food processor or blender and puree the soup until it is smooth, then return the mixture to the pot. Add the diced tomatoes with their juice and the corn, green chilies, and cilantro. Continue to cook the soup over medium heat until it is heated thoroughly.

To serve, ladle the soup into individual bowls and sprinkle tortilla chips on top.

Serves 4

Vegetable Soup

3 T. butter
1 small onion, chopped
1 stalk celery, thinly sliced
2 carrots, peeled and sliced or chopped
1 large potato, peeled and cut into bite-size pieces
2 large tomatoes, peeled, seeded, and chopped
4 cups chicken or vegetable broth
1 tsp. basil

2 zucchini, sliced
½ small head cauliflower or broccoli, broken into
    flowerets (or a combination of the two)
1 cup peas, fresh or frozen
Salt and pepper to taste
Parmesan cheese (optional)

In a large soup pot, melt the butter, then add the onion, celery, and carrots. Cook, stirring occasionally, until the onion is soft and translucent. Add the potato, tomatoes, broth, and basil. Bring the broth to a boil and then reduce the heat, cover, and simmer for 15 minutes.

Add the zucchini and cauliflower or broccoli and simmer, covered, for 10 minutes.

Add the peas and simmer until tender. (This won't take but a few minutes.)

Season to taste with salt and pepper and serve. A bit of Parmesan cheese sprinkled on top of the soup adds a nice garnish if desired.

Serves 4 to 6

Zucchini Soup

1 T. butter
2 cups zucchini, thinly sliced
½ cup onion
1 tsp. lemon juice

2 cups chicken broth
1 cup heavy cream or half-and-half
Salt and pepper to taste

In a soup pot, melt the butter and then add the zucchini and onion and cook until the vegetables are tender, stirring gently and regularly. Add the lemon juice and the chicken broth and bring the broth to a simmer; cook, covered, for about 15 minutes. Reduce the heat slightly and add the cream; heat until thoroughly hot. Add salt and pepper to taste and serve.

Serves 4

Note: *We like to enhance the flavor of this soup by adding a bit of garlic and dill weed. You can also add rosemary or basil.*

A hearty stew is pure comfort food. And because a stew mostly simmers undisturbed until you're ready to serve, it's a boon to busy cooks who don't have time to fuss in the kitchen preparing a meal. Simply cut up some meat and vegetables, add liquid and seasonings, and you're good to go.

For a change of pace, try the Black Beans with Pork and Citrus Sauce. The Five-Hour Beef Stew is perfect for lunch after church on Sunday because it cooks slowly in the oven while you're away. Stonaflesch is an old-fashioned dry stew with few ingredients that is big on taste—and kids love it.

Stew doesn't have to be the same old thing. I chose a variety for you to try. I'm sure you'll find some new favorites here, so get cooking and enjoy!

Beef Stew with Coffee

1 cup flour
1½ tsp. salt
½ tsp. pepper
1 tsp. thyme
3 lbs. beef stew meat, cubed
3 T. oil

5 cups beef broth
1 cup strong brewed coffee
1 T. Worcestershire sauce
1 tsp. paprika
1 tsp. sugar
3 T. catsup

6 potatoes, peeled and quartered
2 small or 1 large onion, quartered
6 carrots, peeled and quartered
½ cup peas, fresh or frozen

Place the flour, salt, pepper, and thyme in a medium mixing bowl or a gallon-sized plastic bag and mix or shake to blend. Add the beef cubes, working in batches, and shake or stir to coat the beef with the flour mixture. You can set the coated pieces on a cookie sheet as you continue coating all the beef cubes.

In a large stockpot, heat the oil and add the beef cubes, browning them on all sides. (You may need to add a bit more oil, especially if you brown the beef in batches.) Next, add all the remaining ingredients except the peas, and simmer, covered, for about 1½ to 2 hours. Add the peas and continue to simmer the stew until the peas are done, about 10 to 15 minutes more.

Serves 6

Note: *When I know I'm going to be making this stew for lunch or dinner, I purposely make extra coffee in the morning. I measure out a cup and put it in the fridge (covered) until I'm ready to make the stew.*

Beef Stew with Dumplings

STEW	DUMPLINGS
3 T. shortening, lard, or oil	1 cup flour
2 lbs. beef stew meat, cubed	1½ tsp. baking powder
2 T. flour	½ tsp. salt
1½ tsp. salt	1 egg
⅛ tsp. pepper	2 to 3 T. milk
1 quart boiling water	1 T. butter or shortening, melted
1 tsp. lemon juice	and cooled slightly

For the stew:

Melt the shortening in a Dutch oven or large, deep skillet with a lid. Add the meat cubes and brown them well on all sides. Sprinkle the flour, salt, and pepper over the meat; add the boiling water and lemon juice and then cover the pot, lower the heat, and simmer for about 3 hours. (Check occasionally to see if additional water is needed.) When you are nearing the end of the simmering time, make the dumplings.

For the dumplings:

In a medium mixing bowl, stir together the flour, baking powder, and salt. In another bowl, combine the egg, milk, and melted butter. Make a well in the center of the dry ingredients and pour the egg mixture into the well. Mix just until incorporated—you don't want to overmix the dough. Drop large spoonfuls of dough into the simmering stew; cover the pot and allow the dumplings to cook without raising the lid for 15 minutes. (You might need a bit more cooking time, especially if the dumplings are on the large side, but it's better to have smaller and more dumplings instead of large ones.) Serve the stew as soon as the dumplings are ready.

Serves 6

Black Beans with Pork and Citrus Sauce

STEW

2 T. olive oil
½ to 1 lb. pork, cubed
2 cloves garlic, minced
1 small onion, chopped
1 large or 2 medium tomatoes, skinned and chopped

3 (15 oz.) cans black beans, rinsed and drained (you can use pinto beans if you prefer)
Beef broth or water (at least a quart)
Salt and pepper to taste
Hot cooked rice for serving

SAUCE

⅓ cup lemon juice
⅓ cup orange juice
½ tsp. cumin
1 tsp. basil
1 tsp. oregano
2 cloves garlic, minced

For the stew:

In a large pot, heat the oil and add the pork. Brown the meat on all sides and then add the garlic, onion, tomatoes, rinsed beans, and enough broth or water to barely cover. Add salt and pepper to taste. Cover the pot with a lid and cook the stew on low heat for several hours so it has a chance to thicken a bit. (Although you can eat it much sooner than that, say, after an hour of cooking time.)

For the citrus sauce:

Combine all the ingredients in a jar with a tight-fitting lid. Shake the jar hard to thoroughly mix the contents. Sometimes the spices want to float on top and the minced garlic likes to drop to the bottom, so I usually use a spoon to mix and scoop the sauce when I'm ready to use it.

To serve:

Place some hot cooked rice in the bottom of individual bowls. Ladle the stew on the rice and then spoon some citrus sauce on top. Don't be shy with the sauce—it's delicious!

Serves 6 to 8

Buffet Beef Cubes with Noodles

1½ lbs. beef chuck, trimmed of fat and cubed	1 T. Worcestershire sauce
2 T. flour	1½ tsp. salt
2 T. shortening	1 tsp. white vinegar
2¼ cups V8 juice	½ tsp. basil
1½ cups onion, diced	¼ tsp. pepper
¼ cup water	1 bay leaf
1 T. sugar	3 cups uncooked egg noodles (page 72)

In a gallon-sized plastic bag, add the meat cubes and flour and shake well to coat the meat.

In a heavy stewpot (enamel-coated cast iron works well for this recipe), melt the shortening and then add the meat and brown on all sides. Add the remaining ingredients to the pot except the uncooked noodles, and simmer, covered, for about 2 hours or until the beef is tender and the sauce is thick like gravy. Stir often to prevent sticking.

Shortly before your mealtime, cook the egg noodles according to the directions on page 72 (you can also use packaged egg noodles). Drain the noodles and add them to the stew. Alternately, you can put some noodles on plates or in bowls and ladle the stew over the top.

Serves 6

Note: *Egg noodles don't expand nearly as much as regular pasta, such as spaghetti noodles. I get a little more than 4 cups of cooked noodles from 3 cups of uncooked egg noodles. Yours might differ, so you may need to experiment with the amount of noodles you cook.*

Chicken Alfredo Stew

SAUCE	STEW
4 T. butter	2 T. oil
4 T. flour	1¼ lbs. boneless, skinless chicken thighs, chunked
2 cups milk	4 cups potatoes, peeled and diced
¾ cup water	1 cup carrots, peeled and diced
1 tsp. dried basil leaves	½ cup corn, fresh or frozen
½ tsp. salt	½ cup peas, fresh or frozen
	Parmesan cheese for serving

For the Alfredo sauce:

Melt the butter in a medium saucepan, then stir in the flour to form a roux. Stirring constantly, gradually whisk the milk into the roux and keep stirring until the mixture begins to bubble and thicken. Add the water, basil, and salt and stir to mix well. Taste and adjust the seasonings; you might need a bit more salt, and you can add some pepper if you desire.

For the stew:

In a large pot, heat the oil; add the chicken pieces and brown them lightly on all sides. Stir in the Alfredo sauce. Next, add the potatoes and carrots and bring everything to a slow simmer. Cover the pot and cook the stew until the potatoes and carrots are tender and the chicken is cooked thoroughly, about 20 to 25 minutes. Add the corn and peas and cook for about 5 to 10 minutes longer or until done. Serve with Parmesan cheese to taste.

Serves 8

Note: *To make this recipe a bit simpler, you can use a (16 oz.) jar of Alfredo sauce in place of the homemade sauce in this recipe. Skip the first three ingredients in the list, but include the water, ½ tsp. basil and the salt when you add the Alfredo sauce to the stew.*

Chicken Goulash

1 whole chicken
2 cups tomatoes, chopped
2 tsp. salt
3 onions, chopped

1 green bell pepper, seeded and chopped
4 potatoes, peeled and cubed
1 to 2 T. paprika
sour cream (optional)

Boil the chicken in a large pot with enough water to cover it fully; cook until tender, about 2½ hours. Remove the chicken from the broth so both can cool faster. When the chicken is cool, remove the meat from the skin and bones and cut the meat into bite-size pieces. Strain off as much fat from the broth as you can.

Return the meat to the strained broth, add the remaining ingredients except the sour cream, and simmer for 1 hour. Taste and adjust the seasonings as desired.

To serve, ladle the stew into individual bowls and top each with a dollop of sour cream.

Serves 6

Chicken, Sweet Potato, and Cabbage Stew

3 cups sweet potatoes, peeled and cubed
2 T. olive oil
1½ lbs. boneless, skinless chicken breasts, cubed
3 cups chicken broth
3 cups cabbage, coarsely shredded
1 (16 oz.) can baby lima beans or butter beans, drained

1 (14½ oz.) can diced tomatoes, undrained
1 cup celery, sliced
1 cup tomato juice
Salt and pepper to taste

Place the cubed sweet potatoes in a saucepan, cover them with water, and bring the water to a boil. Reduce the heat and simmer until the sweet potatoes are almost tender, about 10 to 15 minutes. Drain the water from the sweet potatoes and set them aside for now.

In a stockpot, heat the olive oil and brown the pieces of chicken on all sides. Add the chicken broth and the half-cooked sweet potato cubes and bring to a boil; reduce the heat, add the remaining ingredients, and simmer until the chicken is thoroughly cooked and the sweet potatoes are tender, about 20 to 30 minutes.

Serves 8

Chili Verde

2 T. oil
¾ lb. beef chuck or round roast, cubed
¾ lb. boneless pork shoulder roast, cubed
5 cloves garlic, minced
2 (28 oz.) cans tomatoes, cut up, or 4 (14½ oz.) cans diced tomatoes
8 (4 oz.) cans diced green chilies, drained
1 green bell pepper, chopped
1 cup beef broth
2 tsp. ground cumin
½ tsp. sugar
¼ tsp. ground cloves
3 jalapeño peppers, seeded and chopped (optional)
⅓ cup fresh parsley, snipped

Heat the oil in a large Dutch oven or heavy pot; brown the meat, half at a time, adding garlic to the second half of the browning meat. Drain off the excess fat and return all the meat to the Dutch oven. Add the remaining ingredients except the parsley. Bring the stew to a boil and then turn down the heat, cover the pot, and simmer for 2 hours, stirring occasionally. Uncover the pot and simmer for another 30 minutes or so until the stew has reached its desired consistency. Stir in the parsley just before serving.

Serves 6

Chili Without Beans

1½ lbs. ground beef
2 (14½ oz.) cans diced or stewed tomatoes, undrained
1 (8 oz.) can tomato sauce
1 small onion, chopped
1 green bell pepper, chopped
1 (4 oz.) can chopped green chilies
1 T. chili powder
2 cloves garlic, minced
1 tsp. salt
½ tsp. paprika
¼ tsp. pepper
½ cup fresh minced parsley
Toppings if desired

In a heavy pot, brown the ground beef and then drain the grease. Add the remainder of the ingredients except the parsley. Simmer this chili for about an hour, adding the parsley in the final 10 minutes of cooking time.

Ladle the chili into individual bowls and serve with shredded cheese (Jack, cheddar, or crumbled Cotija), a dollop of sour cream, and sliced green onions if desired. Some people like to serve this over cooked rice.

Serves 6 to 8

Creamy Potato and Vegetable Stew

3 quarts water
8 large potatoes, peeled and cubed
4 to 6 carrots, peeled and sliced or chopped
2 stalks celery, sliced
⅓ cup butter
2 small or 1 large onion, chopped

2 T. flour
1½ tsp. salt
1 tsp. pepper
¼ tsp. paprika
2 cups heavy cream

In a large pot or Dutch oven, add the water, potatoes, carrots, and celery and bring to a boil. Decrease the heat and simmer the stew until the vegetables are just barely tender. Drain the vegetables and set them aside, reserving the liquid in a separate bowl.

In the same pot, melt the butter; add the onions and cook them slowly for about 10 minutes, stirring often, until they are very tender. Add the flour, salt, pepper, and paprika and stir. Gradually add the cream while stirring constantly. Continue stirring for several minutes so the flour doesn't form lumps. Add the vegetables back into the pot and add the reserved liquid a ladleful at a time to get the desired consistency.

Ladle the stew into individual serving bowls. If desired, sprinkle each bowl of stew with a small amount of fresh snipped parsley, a shake of paprika, or diced fresh tomatoes.

Serves 8

Five-Hour Beef Stew

2 lbs. beef stew meat, cubed
3 potatoes, peeled and chunked
3 chopped onions
6 carrots, peeled and thickly sliced
1 cup celery, sliced
1 quart canned tomatoes, or 2 (14½ oz.) cans
   stewed tomatoes

3 T. minute tapioca
½ T. sugar
1 T. salt
1 slice stale bread, torn into bite-size pieces

Mix together all the ingredients in a Dutch oven or a large glass baking dish. Use the Dutch oven lid or a double layer of foil to tightly cover the stew. Bake at 250° for 5 hours. (If you are using a glass baking dish, check after about 4 hours to make sure the stew isn't cooking too quickly. You don't even need to open the foil cover. Just peek around the edges to make sure it doesn't look too dark. If it looks like the stew is done and is getting dark, remove it from the oven and serve.)

Serves 6

Ground Turkey Chili

2 tsp. oil
1 onion, chopped
3 carrots, peeled and sliced or chopped
1 green bell pepper, seeded and chopped
1 cup fresh mushrooms, sliced
1 lb. ground turkey
1 to 2 T. chili powder
2 tsp. oregano
1 tsp. cumin

Pepper to taste
2 (28 oz.) cans crushed tomatoes (or use 2 quarts
   home-canned tomatoes)
1 tsp. hot red pepper sauce (such as Tabasco,
   Cholula, or sriracha)
6 cloves garlic, minced
1 quart home-canned red beans, or 2 (15 oz.) cans
   kidney beans or small red beans, drained
Toppings if desired

In a large stewpot, heat the oil and sauté the onion, carrot, and bell pepper for 3 minutes; add the mushrooms and cook 3 minutes more. Add the turkey, chili powder, oregano, cumin, and pepper and cook, breaking up the ground turkey, until the meat is no longer pink. Add the remaining ingredients, stir well, and simmer over low heat for 30 to 45 minutes, stirring occasionally.

You can garnish individual bowls of chili with shredded cheese, a dollop of sour cream, and some fresh parsley or cilantro if desired.

Serves 8

I-Can't-Cook Stew

Seriously. Don't you have those days when you need to feed the family and don't have the time or the inclination to make a meal? This will take care of those days nicely. Butter some bread and call it dinner.

1 lb. ground beef
2 cans vegetable soup

1 can water or beef broth (use 1½ to 2 cans of water if the soup you are using is condensed)
2 cans ranch-style beans, undrained

In a stewpot, brown the ground beef; drain off fat. Add the remaining ingredients and simmer until the ground beef is cooked through. The size of cans you use doesn't really matter—just use what you have to match the appetites of the people you need to feed.

Serves 6

Lentil and Sweet Potato Stew

1¼ cups dried lentils
6 cups chicken or vegetable broth
2 carrots, peeled and sliced
2 sweet potatoes, peeled and cubed
1 onion, quartered
2 cloves garlic, minced

2 T. tomato paste
1 bay leaf
1 tsp. dried parsley
½ tsp. turmeric
½ tsp. ground cumin
½ tsp. ginger

Rinse and drain the lentils, picking out any debris as you do so. Put the lentils in a stockpot and add all the remaining ingredients. Bring to a boil, then reduce the heat and simmer until the lentils are cooked and the sweet potatoes are tender, about 1 hour. If the stew starts to get too dry, cover it with a lid to finish cooking.

Serves 6

Quick and Easy Taco Stew

1 lb. ground beef
1 medium onion, chunked
1 (14½ oz.) can whole kernel corn, drained,
   or 2 cups fresh or frozen corn
1 (14½ oz.) can diced tomatoes with green chilies,
   undrained

1 (16 oz.) can pinto beans with chili sauce, undrained
1 (10¾ oz.) can condensed tomato soup, undiluted
1 cup water
Tortilla chips, cheese, sour cream, and cilantro
   for garnish

In a stewpot, brown the ground beef, then drain off the fat. Add the remainder of the ingredients and simmer for about 25 to 30 minutes or longer, making sure that the meat is thoroughly cooked before serving.

To serve, ladle the stew into individual bowls and top with tortilla chips and shredded cheese if desired.

Serves 6 to 8

Rabbit Stew

1 rabbit, dressed and cut to pieces
2 cups water
Flour for dredging
1 tsp. salt
¼ tsp. pepper
¼ cup oil
2 onions, sliced

2 cloves garlic, minced
½ cup vinegar
1 (14½ oz.) can stewed or diced tomatoes, undrained
1 (6 oz.) can tomato paste
½ cup vinegar
2 cloves garlic, minced
½ tsp. ground cloves

Place the rabbit pieces in a stockpot and add the water; cover the pot and simmer until the meat is cooked thoroughly and beginning to fall off the bones. Remove the meat and set it aside until it is cool enough to handle. While the meat is cooling, strain the broth and save it to add to the stew. Remove the meat from the bones and cut the meat into large bite-size pieces.

Roll the pieces of meat in flour and sprinkle them with the salt and pepper. Heat the oil in a clean stewpot and fry the floured pieces of meat until they are browned on all sides. Using a slotted spoon, remove the meat and set it aside. In the same pot, cook the onion slices until they are limp and lightly browned. Add the meat and broth to the stewpot along with all the other ingredients. Cover the pot and let the stew simmer for 1 to 1½ hours, adding more water as needed. You can also bake the stew in a covered, ovenproof pot at 350° for 1 to 1½ hours.

Serves 6 to 8

Spicy Fish Stew

1 T. oil
1 cup onion, chopped
¼ cup celery, sliced
1 tsp. chili powder
1½ cups corn, fresh or frozen
1 T. Worcestershire sauce
1 (14½ oz.) can diced tomatoes, undrained

2 cups water
1 lb. white fish, such as rockfish, cod, tilapia,
   or halibut, cut into bite-size pieces
Cayenne pepper to taste
Salt to taste
¼ cup chopped fresh cilantro or parsley
Lemon or lime, cut into wedges, if desired

Heat the oil in a large pot, then add the onion, celery, and chili powder and sauté until the vegetables are tender.

Stir in the corn, Worcestershire sauce, diced tomatoes, and water. Simmer for 10 minutes, then add the fish and cook until the fish is done, about 3 to 5 minutes. Add the cayenne pepper and salt to taste, and stir in the cilantro or parsley just before removing from the heat.

Ladle the stew into individual bowls, and squeeze the juice of one or two lemon or lime wedges over the stew if desired.

Serves 5

Stonaflesch

I ate this all my growing up years. I don't remember a time when it wasn't on our family's menu line-up. As for the name, it's what we've always called it. I had no idea where it came from! But I recently found out it sounds like the German phrase "hour of meat." Go figure!

2 lbs. ground beef	Salt and pepper
10 carrots, peeled and sliced	Paprika
6 large potatoes, peeled and thinly sliced	

This dish is made in layers. It's better to have several thin layers rather than a few thick ones. Ground beef will be your first and your final layer, so portion out your ingredients accordingly.

In a heavy ovenproof pot, cover the entire bottom of the pot with a layer of raw ground beef, breaking apart the beef into little pieces as you work. Next add a layer of carrots and then a layer of potatoes. Top each potato layer with salt and pepper and continue layering. Once you've added the final layer of beef, sprinkle paprika over the top and cover the pot with a tight-fitting lid.

Bake at 350° for at least an hour or until the carrots and potatoes are cooked through and tender. You can also cook the Stonaflesch at 250° for 3 to 4 hours, but you'll need to check occasionally to make sure the bottom doesn't scorch.

Serves 8

Note: *This is a dry stew. In spite of its simplicity and very few ingredients, it's a soothing and tasty meal on a cold winter day. It is also a very forgiving dish: you can use less meat or more potatoes or carrots. For instance, I almost always use much less ground beef because I'm frugal. (Less than a pound of ground beef to feed an entire family!) One last mention: kids generally love this dish.*

Three-Bean Meatless Chili

1 quart jar tomatoes, undrained (or 1 [28 oz.] can crushed tomatoes)

1 pint jar white beans, drained (or 1 [15 oz.] can, drained)

1 pint jar kidney beans, drained (or 1 [15 oz.] can, drained)

1 pint jar black beans, drained (or 1 [15 oz.] can, drained)

1 (10 oz.) can mild enchilada sauce

1 cup tomato sauce (½-pint jar or an 8 oz. can)

1 (4½ oz.) can chopped mild green chilies

1 red bell pepper, seeded and diced

½ cup onion, diced

2 to 3 tsp. chili powder (depending on how spicy you like it)

1 tsp. oregano

½ tsp. cumin

Toppings if desired

Stir together all the ingredients in a large pot and bring it to a boil. Lower the heat, cover the pot, and simmer, stirring occasionally, for at least 30 minutes. An hour of cooking time is best because it will better meld the flavors.

To serve, ladle chili into individual bowls and top with shredded cheddar cheese, a dollop of sour cream, chopped avocados, or broken tortilla chips if desired.

Serves 6 to 8

Venison Stew

¼ cup olive oil

2 to 3 lbs. venison or elk steaks, rinsed, dried, and cubed

1 T. salt

Pepper to taste

6 cups water

2 T. beef granules or 3 beef bouillon cubes

2 T. Worcestershire sauce

1 (1 oz.) envelope dry onion soup mix

2 tsp. garlic, minced

4 potatoes, peeled and cubed (or use about 6 small red potatoes and quarter them, leaving the peels on)

6 carrots, peeled and thickly sliced

4 stalks celery, sliced

3 T. cornstarch

Heat the oil in a Dutch oven or heavy pot; add the venison cubes and brown them on all sides, sprinkling them with salt and pepper while browning. Add the water, beef bouillon, Worcestershire sauce, and dry soup mix. Cover the pot and simmer the stew for 1½ hours.

Stir in the garlic, potatoes, carrots, and celery and continue to simmer until the vegetables are tender, about another 20 minutes.

Remove ½ cup of the stew broth and mix in the cornstarch, whisking vigorously so it doesn't clump. Gradually pour the cornstarch mixture back into the stew, stirring constantly, and continue to simmer until the broth thickens.

Serves 6 to 8

Tomato
sauce
9/25/21

Tomato
sauce
9/25/21

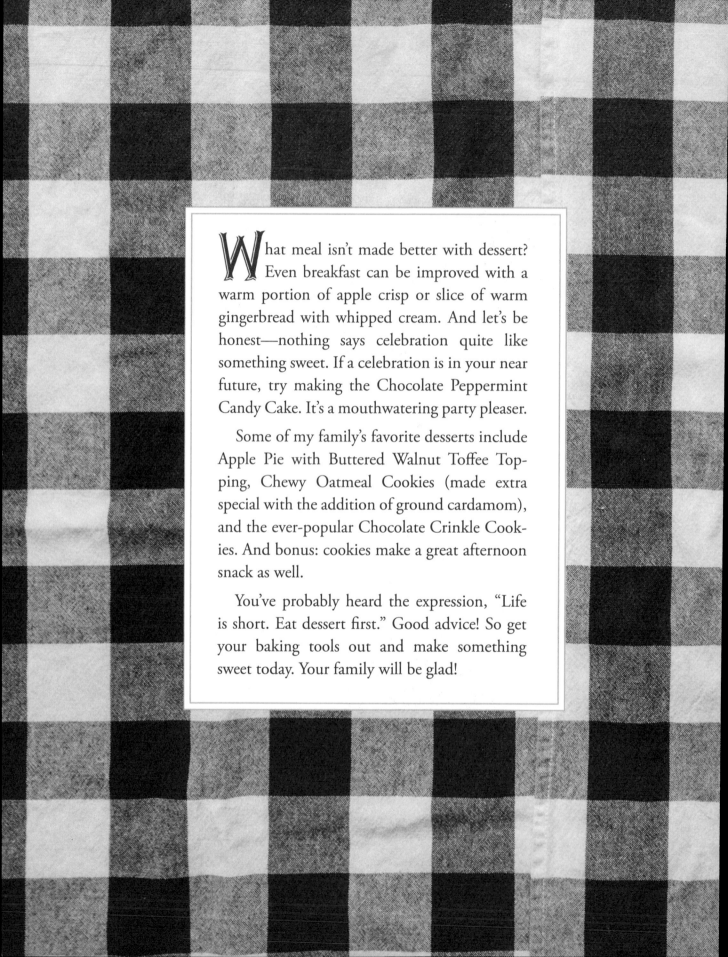

What meal isn't made better with dessert? Even breakfast can be improved with a warm portion of apple crisp or slice of warm gingerbread with whipped cream. And let's be honest—nothing says celebration quite like something sweet. If a celebration is in your near future, try making the Chocolate Peppermint Candy Cake. It's a mouthwatering party pleaser.

Some of my family's favorite desserts include Apple Pie with Buttered Walnut Toffee Topping, Chewy Oatmeal Cookies (made extra special with the addition of ground cardamom), and the ever-popular Chocolate Crinkle Cookies. And bonus: cookies make a great afternoon snack as well.

You've probably heard the expression, "Life is short. Eat dessert first." Good advice! So get your baking tools out and make something sweet today. Your family will be glad!

Mama's Pie Crust

As you might have guessed, this is an old family recipe. My mama called it "Mama's Pie Crust" because she originally got it from her mom!

SINGLE CRUST	**DOUBLE CRUST**
1½ cups sifted flour	2 cups sifted flour
½ tsp. salt	1 tsp. salt
½ cup shortening or lard	⅔ cup shortening or lard

If you plan to prebake the crust, preheat the oven to 425°.

To make the dough:

In a teacup or small bowl, make a paste with ¼ cup of the flour (⅓ cup if making double crust) and 3 tablespoons of water (¼ cup water for double crust). Set it in the refrigerator. In a medium mixing bowl, add the salt to the remaining flour and whisk to distribute the salt throughout. Cut the shortening into the flour until it forms crumbs the size of small peas. Add the water paste to the flour mixture and mix just until the dough comes together. Form the dough into a ball and turn it out on a floured surface. (If you are making a double crust, work with half the dough at a time.) Roll the crust into a circle that is about ⅛-inch thick.

To prebake the crust:

Line a pie pan with one pie shell. Line the pie shell with foil or parchment paper and fill it with a cup of raw white rice or small white beans. The weight from the rice or beans will keep the bottom of the crust from puffing up while baking. You can save the rice or beans to use for future pie crusts by cooling them completely and then storing them in an airtight, marked container. Bake the pie crust for 12 to 15 minutes or until golden.

Makes 1 or 2 pie crusts

To keep your pie dough from sticking while you roll it out, ice your countertop. Place ice cubes into a gallon freezer bag along with a small amount of water to make it lie flat, seal the bag, and set it on the counter until the surface is cold. Another great choice for a nonstick surface is marble—but marble is heavy, so a good substitute is granite. Don't have a marble or granite countertop? You can buy a slab of either one in many kitchen shops.

Apple Crisp

During apple season, this is an easy go-to recipe when you want a quick and satisfying dessert. Get a head start by mixing up several batches of the crumb topping ahead of time, put them in tightly covered canning jars or plastic bags, and refrigerate them until needed. They'll keep just fine for a week or so.

1 cup brown sugar, packed	½ cup cold butter
1 cup flour	2½ lbs. apples (about 7 or 8)
2 tsp. cinnamon, divided	2 tsp. lemon juice

Preheat the oven to 350°.

Lightly grease or butter a 9-inch square baking dish and set it aside.

In a small mixing bowl, stir together sugar, flour, and 1 tsp. cinnamon. With a pastry blender, two forks, or your fingers, cut in the butter until the mixture is crumbly; set aside.

In another mixing bowl, peel, core, and thinly slice the apples. Gently mix in the remaining teaspoon of cinnamon and the lemon juice. Spread the apples in the prepared baking dish and sprinkle the crumb mixture evenly over the top.

Bake, uncovered, for 50 to 60 minutes or until the apples are tender and the crumb topping is golden and crisp. Let the dish cool for about 30 minutes before serving.

Serves 4 to 6

Apple Crumb Pie

This is a tasty variation of the more usual top-crust apple pie. It doesn't take any more time and is a great change of pace.

6 apples suitable for pie	¾ cup flour
1 cup sugar, divided	⅓ cup butter
1 tsp. cinnamon	1 unbaked pie shell (see Mama's Pie Crust, page 191)

Preheat the oven to 425°. Lay out the unbaked pie shell in a pie plate and set aside.

Peel and core the apples and cut them into thin slices. In a small bowl, make a mixture of ½ cup sugar and the cinnamon and then sprinkle it over the apples, gently mixing. Put the apple mixture into the unbaked pie shell.

Using your fingers, blend the remaining ½ cup sugar with the flour and butter to make coarse crumbs. Sprinkle the crumbs over the apples and bake. After 10 minutes at 425°, reduce the oven to 350° and continue baking for 35 minutes or until the pie is done.

Serves 6 to 8

When choosing apples for baking it's a great idea to ask the advice of local growers or grocers. They'll have good input. Here is my list of apples that hold up well to baking: Braeburn, Cortland, Gala, Golden Delicious, Granny Smith, Honeycrisp, Jonagold, Jonathan, McIntosh, and Northern Spy.

Apple Pie with Buttered Walnut Toffee Topping

This recipe gives a whole new meaning to apple pie. It's delectable. Try topping the pie with pecans instead of walnuts for a tasty variation.

PIE
Pastry for a 2-crust pie (see Mama's Pie Crust, page 191)
⅓ cup light corn syrup
3 T. sugar
1 T. butter, melted
1 T. quick-cooking tapioca
1 tsp. cinnamon
½ tsp. nutmeg
¼ tsp. salt
4 to 6 apples (I use Granny Smiths, but any good pie apple will work)

TOPPING
¼ slightly heaping cup brown sugar
¼ cup chopped walnuts or pecans
3 T. light corn syrup
3 T. butter, melted
2 T. flour
1 tsp. vanilla extract
2 T. flour
¼ tsp. cinnamon

Preheat the oven to 425°.

Roll out half of the dough and line a large pie plate. (Use at least a 9.5-inch size, or you'll have boil-over issues. I personally use a large, extra deep pie plate and don't have boil-overs.) Set it aside for now.

In a large mixing bowl, combine the corn syrup, sugar, melted butter, tapioca, cinnamon, nutmeg, and salt. Let this mixture sit for 10 minutes. Meanwhile, peel, core, and thinly slice the apples. Add the sliced apples to the pie mixture and stir to coat, then pour the filling into the pie shell. Roll out the top crust and place it on top of the apple mixture. Crimp the edges, making sure that there is a ridge all around the edge of the crust. This will be very helpful when you add the toffee topping later on. Make some slashes in the top crust to allow the steam to vent.

Bake the pie at 425° for 10 minutes and then reduce the heat to 350° and bake for another 30 minutes.

While the pie is baking, mix together all the buttered walnut toffee topping ingredients in a bowl.

Remove the pie from the oven after the above baking time is complete and pour the topping over the top crust. (You'll find that the topping doesn't "pour" too well, but just do your best to cover the whole area.) Immediately return the pie to the oven, still set at 350°, and bake for 5 more minutes. If you are worried about the pie boiling over, try placing a large cookie sheet underneath to catch any drips.

Remove the pie from the oven and place it on a rack to cool. It needs to cool until almost room temperature before you slice it so the butter toffee coating has a chance to harden.

Serves 8

Applesauce Loaf Cake

CAKE

1 cup brown sugar
¼ cup butter, room temperature
Pinch of salt
1 tsp. cinnamon
½ tsp. cloves
Pinch of nutmeg

1 cup applesauce
1 tsp. baking soda, mixed with
  just enough warm water to
  dissolve
2 cups flour
1 cup raisins, more or less
Chopped nuts (optional)

FROSTING

1 cup powdered sugar
1 to 2 T. butter, room temperature
1 tsp. water

Preheat the oven to 350°.

For the cake:

Cream together the sugar, butter, salt, and spices. Add the applesauce, dissolved baking soda, and flour; mix well. Add the raisins and mix well again.

Pour the batter into a greased loaf pan. Bake for 45 to 50 minutes or until done, then cool the cake to room temperature.

For the frosting:

Beat together the sugar and butter, adding water if necessary to get the desired consistency. Frost the cake after it has cooled.

I usually use fewer raisins, and sometimes I add some chopped nuts.

Serves 8

Blueberry Custard Pie

PIE
1 baked pie shell (see Mama's Pie Crust, page 191)
1 cup sugar, divided
5 T. cornstarch, divided
⅛ tsp. cinnamon
3 cups blueberries, fresh or frozen
¼ cup orange juice
⅛ tsp. salt
1¼ cups milk
3 eggs, divided

TOPPING
3 egg whites (from the divided eggs
   used in the custard)
¼ tsp. cream of tartar
6 T. sugar

For the pie:

In a large saucepan, combine ½ cup of the sugar, 3 T. of the cornstarch, and the cinnamon. Stir in the blueberries and orange juice. Bring the fruit to a boil over medium heat and cook, stirring until thickened (about 2 minutes). Remove the pan from the heat and set it aside.

In another large saucepan, combine the salt with the remaining sugar and cornstarch. Whisk in the milk until it is smooth, then cook over medium heat, stirring constantly, until thickened. Continue to cook, stirring all the while, for 2 minutes more. Remove the custard from the heat, cover the pan, and set it aside.

Separate the eggs, and reserve the whites to use with the meringue. Stir a small amount of the hot custard mixture into the egg yolks. Stirring constantly, slowly add the egg yolk mixture back into the custard. Return the pan to the heat and bring the custard to a simmer. Cook, stirring constantly, for 2 minutes longer, then remove it from heat, cover, and set it aside.

Pour the blueberry mixture into the baked pie shell, and top with custard mixture. Set aside while you prepare the meringue. Meanwhile, preheat the oven to 350°.

For the meringue topping:

In a large mixing bowl, beat the egg whites and cream of tartar at high speed until soft peaks form. Gradually add the sugar, 1 tablespoon at a time, beating well after each addition. The meringue is ready when it appears glossy and somewhat stiff, and peaks form when the beaters are raised. Spread the meringue over the custard and use a spoon to pull it up into attractive points. Be careful to bring the meringue all the way to the edges of the crust to seal in the blueberry filling. Bake the pie for 12 to 15 minutes or until the meringue is a light golden brown. (Watch carefully because the meringue can quickly go from perfect to dark.)

Serve at room temperature. Meringue doesn't take well to refrigeration, so plan to eat it the same day.

Serves 6 to 8

Butterscotch Pie with Meringue Topping

3 egg yolks (reserve the egg whites for the meringue topping)
¼ cup flour
2 cups milk, divided
Pinch of salt
1 cup firmly packed brown sugar

¼ cup butter
½ tsp. vanilla extract
1 pie shell, baked and cooled (see Mama's Pie Crust, page 191)
Meringue topping (see the Blueberry Custard Pie recipe on the previous page)

In a small bowl, beat the egg yolks well and set them aside.

In a large mixing bowl, combine the flour and 1 cup of the milk, mixing until smooth. Add the egg yolks and salt and mix well again. Add the remaining milk and thoroughly blend.

In a medium saucepan over medium-low heat, stir the brown sugar and butter until the butter melts and the sugar dissolves. Continue stirring for 2 minutes longer, then begin slowly adding the flour mixture, stirring constantly the entire time. Continue to stir until the mixture is thickened—don't rush this step and keep the heat low. Remove the pan from the heat and add the vanilla. Continue to stir the butterscotch syrup while it cools to barely warm and then pour it into the prepared pie shell.

Preheat the oven to 350°. Prepare the meringue topping as described in the previous recipe, adding in ½ teaspoon of vanilla with the egg whites.

Carefully spread the meringue all the way to the edges of the crust to seal in the butterscotch filling. Bake the pie for 12 to 15 minutes and serve at room temperature on the same day.

Serves 6 to 8

To keep your brown sugar from getting hard, use a clean shard of terra cotta that has been soaked in water. Place the wet shard into the top of the brown sugar and tightly close the top of the container. Each time you use the brown sugar, take out the shard and resoak it in water while you measure out the amount of sugar to be used. (Kitchen and specialty stores sell pieces of decorative terra cotta that are specially made for using in your brown sugar containers.)

Chewy Oatmeal Cookies

1 cup butter, room temperature

1 cup granulated sugar, plus a bit more for rolling

1 cup brown sugar

2 eggs

1 tsp. vanilla extract

2 cups flour

1 tsp. baking soda

1 scant tsp. salt

1½ tsp. ground cinnamon

¼ tsp. ground cardamom

¼ tsp. ground nutmeg

3 cups rolled oats

In a large mixing bowl, beat together the butter and sugars. Add the eggs one at a time, beating well after each addition. Stir in the vanilla.

In another, smaller bowl, combine the flour, baking soda, salt, and spices. Add the dry ingredients to the creamed mixture and stir well. Add the oats and stir well again. Cover the bowl and chill the dough in the refrigerator for at least an hour.

When you are ready to bake, preheat the oven to 375°.

Form the dough into 1-inch balls and roll the balls in granulated sugar. Place the dough balls 2 inches apart on greased cookie sheets. Flatten them slightly. (Instead of rolling the dough balls in sugar, you can place them on the greased cookie sheets and then dip a fork into sugar and use it to flatten the cookies slightly, running the fork across the tops to release the sugar.)

Bake for 8 to 10 minutes.

Makes about 3 dozen cookies

Refrigerate your cookie dough between batches to make the cookie dough easier to handle when you're ready to shape and bake.

Chocolate Crinkle Cookies

½ cup shortening
1⅔ cups sugar
2 tsp. vanilla extract
2 eggs
2 (1 oz.) squares unsweetened baking
  chocolate, melted

2 cups all-purpose flour, sifted before measuring
2 tsp. baking powder
½ tsp. salt
⅓ cup milk
Powdered sugar

Thoroughly cream together the shortening, sugar, and vanilla. Beat in the eggs and then the chocolate. Sift together the dry ingredients and then alternately add the dry ingredients and the milk to the creamed mixture, blending well after each addition. Chill the dough for 2 to 3 hours.

Preheat the oven to 350°.

Form the chilled dough into 1-inch balls, then roll them in powdered sugar. Place the dough balls 2 to 3 inches apart on greased cookie sheets. Bake for about 15 minutes or until the cookies are cooked through but not too crispy.

Makes about 3 dozen cookies

Chocolate Oatmeal Revel Bars

DOUGH
1 cup butter
2 cups brown sugar
2 eggs
3 cups rolled oats
2½ cups flour
1 tsp. baking soda
½ tsp. salt

FILLING
2 cups chocolate chips
1½ cups sweetened condensed milk
1 T. butter
2 tsp. vanilla extract
1 cup walnut pieces (optional)

Preheat the oven to 350°.

For the dough:

Cream together the butter and sugar. Add the eggs and beat well. Mix together the rolled oats, flour, baking soda, and salt, and then gradually add to the creamed mixture, beating well after each addition.

For the filling:

In a medium saucepan, mix together all the filling ingredients except the walnuts. Cook over medium-low heat, stirring often, until the chocolate is completely melted. Remove from the heat and stir in the walnuts, if using.

Spread about ⅔ of the dough evenly across the bottom of an ungreased 10 x 15 x 1-inch baking pan (or you can use a 9 x 13-inch pan, but you may need to bake the revel bars for 1 to 3 minutes longer). Using a rubber spatula, scrape the filling onto the dough in the pan, spreading evenly. Dot the top with the remaining dough.

Bake for about 25 minutes or until the top is golden. Cool to allow the chocolate to set before cutting the bars.

Makes about 18 bars

Chocolate Peppermint Candy Cake

I hold off until the holidays to make this with candy canes. Every bite is worth the wait. The candy caramelizes on the bottom, and the crunchy, minty taste is delightful!

CAKE
⅔ cup butter, room temperature
1⅔ cups granulated sugar
3 eggs
2 cups flour
⅔ cup cocoa powder
1¼ tsp. baking soda
¼ tsp. baking powder
1 tsp. salt
1⅓ cups milk
½ cup crushed peppermint candy canes
   (or other hard peppermint candy)

FROSTING
½ cup butter
½ cup cocoa powder
3⅔ cups powdered sugar
7 T. milk
1 tsp. vanilla extract
1 T. crushed candy canes

Preheat the oven to 350°. Grease and flour two 9-inch round cake pans; set aside for now.

For the cake:

In a large mixing bowl, cream together the butter, sugar, and eggs until they are well mixed and smooth; then beat on high speed for 3 minutes more.

Mix together the flour, cocoa powder, baking soda, baking powder, and salt. Alternately add the dry ingredients and the milk to the butter mixture, blending well after each addition. Blend in the crushed candy canes.

Spread the batter evenly between the two cake pans and bake for 35 minutes. Cool the cakes for 10 minutes before slipping them from the pans, then allow them to cool completely.

For the frosting:

In a medium saucepan, melt the butter; stirring constantly. Stir in the cocoa powder and cook for about 1 minute until smooth; remove from the heat. Beat in the powdered sugar and milk and continue beating (I do this by hand with a large wooden spoon or rotary eggbeater) until the mixture is smooth and of spreadable consistency; add the vanilla and crushed candy canes and beat again until smooth.

Once the cake is cooled, spread frosting on top of one layer, then stack the second layer on top of the first and spread frosting atop the second layer and all around the sides of the cake.

Serves 8

Crumb Pie

This is an old-time recipe with only a few ingredients. But it really hits the spot when you have a sweet tooth that needs attention!

2 cups flour
1 heaping cup brown sugar
1 tsp. baking soda
1½ T. shortening

½ cup buttermilk or sour cream
Small pinch of salt
1 (9-inch) unbaked pie shell (see Mama's Pie Crust, page 191)

Preheat the oven to 375°. Line a pie pan with the pie crust dough.

Mix together the flour, brown sugar, and baking soda. Cut in the shortening and blend well. Add the buttermilk or sour cream and rub the mixture with your hands until coarse crumbs form. Place the crumbs into the pie shell. Bake for 30 to 40 minutes or until the crust is baked through and the crumbs are golden brown.

Serves 8

Custard "Chess" Pie

Classic. I love to put sweetened whipped cream on top, but it's just as good plain and slightly warm.

4 eggs
½ cup sugar
¼ tsp. salt
1 tsp. vanilla extract

2½ cups scalded milk
1 (9-inch) unbaked pie crust (see Mama's Pie Crust, page 191)

Preheat the oven to 475°. Line a pie pan with the pie crust dough.

In a large bowl, beat the eggs; add the sugar, salt, and vanilla and mix thoroughly. While stirring, slowly pour the scalded milk into the egg and sugar mixture, and then immediately pour this custard into your pie crust. Place the pie in the oven and immediately reduce the heat to 425°. Bake for 35 minutes or until a knife inserted halfway between the center and the edge of the pie comes out clean. Check the pie about halfway through the baking time and turn the oven down to 375° if the crust seems to be getting too dark.

Serves 8

Fruit Cream Pie

You can use almost any fruit for this pie. My favorites are blackberry, blueberry, cherry, currant, raspberry, and strawberry.

1 (9 inch) unbaked pie shell (see Mama's Pie Crust, page 191)
½ cup sugar
1 tsp. flour

½ tsp. salt
3 eggs, beaten
2½ cups milk
½ to ¾ cup fruit

Preheat the oven to 350°. Line a pie pan with the pie shell and set aside.

If using, pit the cherries and cut the strawberries into smaller pieces.

In a large heatproof mixing bowl, stir together the sugar, flour, and salt. Add the beaten eggs and stir again.

Bring the milk to almost boiling and then slowly add it to the egg mixture, stirring constantly. Pour it into the unbaked pie shell and sprinkle the fruit over the top. Bake at 350° for about 45 minutes or until the custard is set. Cool the pie completely before serving.

You can serve this plain or top it with meringue or sweetened whipped cream (page 33).

Gingerbread

½ cup boiling water
½ cup butter or shortening
½ cup brown sugar
½ cup molasses
¼ cup honey
1 egg, well beaten
1½ cups flour

½ tsp. salt
½ tsp. baking powder
½ tsp. baking soda
¾ tsp. ginger
¾ tsp. cinnamon
¼ tsp. allspice

Preheat the oven to 350°.

Pour the boiling water over the butter; add the brown sugar, molasses, honey, and egg and beat well.

Sift together the dry ingredients; gradually add this to the molasses mixture and beat until the batter is smooth. Grease an 8-inch square pan and pour the batter into the pan; bake for 25 minutes or until done.

This is great served plain, but it's even better when served slightly warm with whipped cream on top.

Serves 9

Sand Tarts

1 cup butter
¾ cup powdered sugar, more or less, divided
1 tsp. vanilla extract

2 cups flour
1 cup chopped walnuts or pecans

Preheat the oven to 325°.

In a large mixing bowl, beat the butter until it is light and smooth. Add ½ cup powdered sugar and the vanilla and beat well again. Add the flour and mix until blended, then stir in the nuts.

Shape the dough into a flattened ball. Wrap it tightly in plastic wrap and refrigerate it until cold, about 45 minutes.

Line cookie sheets with parchment paper. Shape the dough into 1-inch balls and place them on the prepared cookie sheets, about an inch apart. Bake for 20 minutes or until golden brown and baked through. They will flatten slightly but still be rounded.

Place the remaining dough back into the refrigerator to keep cold until you are ready to bake the next batch. While the first batch of cookies is baking, sift ¼ cup powdered sugar into a bowl. When the cookies are removed from the oven and while still warm, roll them in the powdered sugar and cool them on wire racks.

Makes about 4 dozen sand tarts

Shoofly Pie

1 (9 inch) unbaked pie crust (see Mama's Pie Crust, page 191)

CRUMBS
½ cup butter or shortening
1½ cups flour
1 cup brown sugar
½ tsp. cinnamon

SYRUP
½ cup molasses
1 tsp. baking soda
1 cup boiling water
⅛ tsp. salt
Pinch each of nutmeg, ginger, cinnamon, and cloves

Preheat the oven to 450°. Line a pie pan with the unbaked crust and set it aside.

With your fingers or a fork, mix together all the crumb ingredients until coarse crumbs form; set aside.

Make the syrup in a heatproof saucepan or mixing bowl: Stir the baking soda into the molasses to dissolve; add the boiling water, salt, and spices and stir well.

Pour one-third of the syrup into the bottom of the pie shell and then add one-third of the crumbs. Repeat these layers twice, ending with the crumbs.

Place the pie into the oven and immediately turn down the heat to 350°. Bake for 30 to 35 minutes or until the crumbs and crust are golden.

Serves 6 to 8

Snickerdoodles

1¾ cups sugar, divided
½ cup butter, softened to room temperature
 (do not use margarine)
1 tsp. vanilla extract
2 eggs

2¾ cups all-purpose flour
1 tsp. cream of tartar
½ tsp. baking soda
¼ tsp. salt
1 T. cinnamon

Preheat oven to 400°.

In a large bowl, cream together 1½ cups sugar and the butter until they are light and fluffy. Mix in the vanilla and eggs and set aside.

In a separate bowl, combine the flour, cream of tartar, baking soda, and salt. Stir the dry ingredients into the wet ingredients and blend until well mixed.

In a small bowl, combine the remaining ¼ cup sugar with the cinnamon. Shape the dough into 1-inch balls and roll them in the cinnamon sugar. Place them on ungreased cookie sheets and bake for 8 to 10 minutes or until the edges are just beginning to brown. Remove the cookies from the cookie sheets and place them on wire racks or a parchment-paper covered work surface to cool.

Makes about 3½ dozen cookies

Keep an aloe vera plant in your kitchen. When you accidentally cut your finger or burn your hand, soothe the injury by immediately snapping off a piece of succulent leaf and rubbing the wound with the antibacterial gel that oozes out.

Soft Molasses Cookies

1 cup butter, room temperature
1½ cups sugar
½ cup molasses
2 eggs
4 cups flour
½ tsp. salt

2¼ tsp. baking soda
2 tsp. ginger
1 tsp. cloves
1½ tsp. cinnamon
Extra sugar, for rolling

Cream together the butter and sugar. Add the molasses and eggs and beat well. Add the flour, salt, baking soda, and spices and beat again. Chill the dough, covered, for at least 30 minutes. Roll the dough into balls and then roll the balls in sugar and place them on ungreased cookie sheets.

Preheat the oven to 350° and bake for 10 or 11 minutes. Do not overbake—because the dough is already dark, you have to trust the timer. Remove the cookies to wire racks to cool. They will continue to firm up while cooling.

Makes about 4 dozen cookies

Walnut Brownies

3 (1 oz.) squares unsweetened chocolate
1 cup butter
2 cups sugar
¼ tsp. salt

1 T. vanilla extract
4 eggs
1 cup all-purpose flour
1 cup chopped walnuts

Preheat the oven to 350°.

In a medium saucepan, melt the chocolate squares and butter together over low heat, stirring constantly. Pour the melted chocolate into a large bowl and stir in the sugar, salt, and vanilla. Beat until well blended. Whisk in the eggs. Stir in the flour until just combined, and fold in the chopped walnuts. Pour the mixture into a greased 9 x 13-inch baking pan and bake for 35 minutes. Cool completely before cutting into bars.

Make about 12 brownies

Take advantage of sunny days, even in winter, by using a solar oven. Think of the solar oven as an eco-friendly slow cooker. If you're handy, you can make your own solar oven, or easily find them for sale online. Choose from the casserole, stew, or soup recipes in this book as a great first place to start.

INDEX

INDEX OF TIPS

ABOUT THE AUTHOR

Georgia Varozza, author of *The Homestead Canning Cookbook* and *The Homestead Sourdough Cookbook*, enjoys teaching people how to prepare and preserve healthy foods, live simply, and get the most from what they have. She is a writer and editor and lives in the Pacific Northwest.

Enjoy More Mouthwatering Recipes
from Georgia's Homestead to Yours

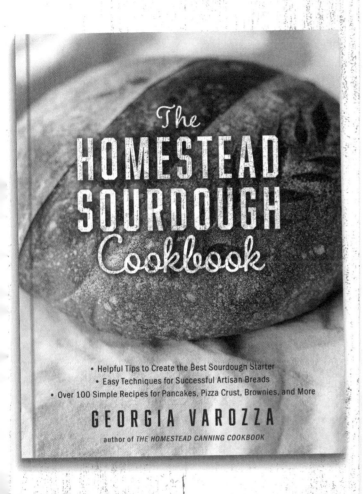

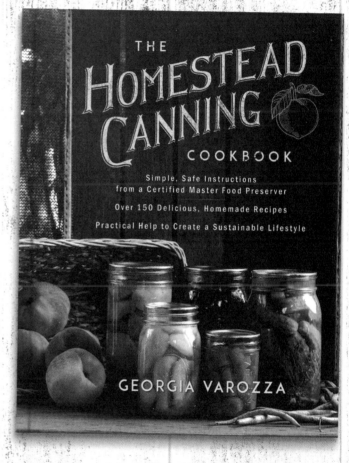

Gain the know-how to bake delicious sourdough breads, biscuits, bagels, buns, and more.

Learn how to safely and successfully can fruit, vegetables, meat, soups, sauces, and more (recipes included).

Discover more great cookbooks at **harvesthousepublishers.com**

Cover and interior design by Dugan Design Group
Photographs by Jay Eads
Interior illustrations © Brigantine Designs / Mighty Deals

For bulk or special sales, please call 1-800-547-8979.
Email: Customerservice@hhpbooks.com

 ® TEN PEAKS PRESS is a trademark of The Hawkins Children's LLC. Harvest House Publishers, Inc., is the exclusive licensee of this trademark.

Some material previously published in *99 Amish Soups and Stews*; *99 Breads, Rolls, and Muffins*; and *99 Favorite Amish Recipes*.

The Homestead-to-Table Cookbook
Copyright © 2023 by Georgia Varozza
Published by Ten Peaks Press, an imprint of Harvest House Publishers
Eugene, Oregon 97408

ISBN 978-0-7369-8736-3 (pbk.)
ISBN 978-0-7369-8737-0 (eBook)

Library of Congress Control Number: 2022944836

Printed in the United States of America

23 24 25 26 27 28 29 30 31 / VP / 10 9 8 7 6 5 4 3 2 1